A Bad Woman's Story
A Translation of *Buri Aurat ki Katha*

A Bad Woman's Story
A Translation of *Buri Aurat ki Katha*

KISHWAR NAHEED

Translated by
Durdana Soomro

OXFORD
UNIVERSITY PRESS

OXFORD
UNIVERSITY PRESS

Great Clarendon Street, Oxford OX2 6DP

Oxford University Press is a department of the University of Oxford.
It furthers the University's objective of excellence in research, scholarship,
and education by publishing worldwide in

Oxford New York

Auckland Cape Town Dar es Salaam Hong Kong Karachi
Kuala Lumpur Madrid Melbourne Mexico City Nairobi
New Delhi Shanghai Taipei Toronto

with offices in

Argentina Austria Brazil Chile Czech Republic France Greece
Guatemala Hungary Italy Japan Poland Portugal Singapore
South Korea Switzerland Turkey Ukraine Vietnam

Oxford is a registered trade mark of Oxford University Press
in the UK and in certain other countries

© Oxford University Press 2009

The moral rights of the author have been asserted

First published 2009

Originally published in Urdu by Sang-e-Meel Publishers, Lahore under the title
Buri Aurat ki Katha by Kishwar Naheed in 2003

All rights reserved. No part of this publication may be reproduced, translated,
stored in a retrieval system, or transmitted, in any form or by any means,
without the prior permission in writing of Oxford University Press.
Enquiries concerning reproduction should be sent to
Oxford University Press at the address below.

This book is sold subject to the condition that it shall not, by way
of trade or otherwise, be lent, re-sold, hired out or otherwise circulated
without the publisher's prior consent in any form of binding or cover
other than that in which it is published and without a similar condition
including this condition being imposed on the subsequent purchaser.

ISBN 978-0-19-547737-5

Typeset in Adobe Garamond Pro
Printed in Pakistan by
Pixel Grafix, Karachi.
Published by
Ameena Saiyid, Oxford University Press
No. 38, Sector 15, Korangi Industrial Area, PO Box 8214
Karachi-74900, Pakistan.

For my sons
Mizo and Faisal

Contents

	page
To My Readers	ix
1. First Stage	1
2. First Step	15
3. First Prostration	27
4. First Idol	39
5. First Appearance	57
6. First Slip	71
7. Mahlaqa's Tale	89
8. At Meera Bai's Feet	109
9. The Birth of Yashodhara	127
10. Uncrowned Zarrin	137
11. Discreet Laila	149
12. The Woman with the Whip	161
13. Sana on the Gallows	171
14. Eve and the Son of Adam	183
Glossary	189

To My Readers!

Ashkabad—one evening my Egyptian friend and I were talking about the changes taking place in our respective courtyards and countries. He laughed and said: 'I too used to talk like you. My mother also wore the *burqa* but now my daughter wears a bikini!'

This was twenty years ago. Today I am sitting in Italy writing my story. In Spain one of my daughters-in-law wears shorts and in America my other daughter-in-law wears skirts. My nieces are working on their doctorates in America, while my mother used to go out in a palanquin!

The manner in which society in the subcontinent has changed itself since 1940 and the impact of these changes on our lanes, neighbourhoods, homes, and minds—creating cobwebs in some places and opening windows in others—all these are tales that need to be told.

This narrative is not tied to any calendar nor is it the charting of a journey up the ladder of life. There is a painting of Van Gogh titled 'Shoes'—whose are they? And does it even matter? This story too is not that of an individual but of our whole society where important issues are overlooked but small meannesses remembered. As Saint-John Perse says, this is the story of the streetwalker who says a prayer in her grief, challenges those who are on the road, and walks with a prince or a dagger in her arms.

In a society where the masses are like burnt out embers in a hearth and, like the Nigerian novelist Ekwensi, have witnessed twenty-seven changes of government in the fifty years of their existence, there, like Kundera, in order to give voice to the nation's tragedy new genres and new creative expressions have to be found.

Margaret Atwood and Maya Angelou have declared self-narrative in the form of monologue as the new novel in which plot is not necessary: the subtext itself can make a novel.

But this debate is not my problem. Nor is it my problem as to what can be published and what cannot be published. After all Kafka was not published in Czechoslovakia; Lao She was silenced during Mao Zedong's time; now there is no mention of Mao Zedong. Lenin's tomb is gone, the Berlin Wall has fallen, the entire geography of Africa, Asia and Europe, its whole history, has changed. Has the enigma of existence in this world also changed!

After the publication of the photographs of the naked, crazed women of Bosnia the debate as to what can or cannot be published is dead and buried.

The famous painter Alberti would go to the other artists pretending to be a novice and question them about their art. I too have peeked into the courtyards of houses and may even at some point have said: 'The emperor is naked.'

Chapter One
First Stage

Who did Eve narrate her story to?
    To Adam—he proclaimed that I had emerged from his rib;

To God—His books branded me a temptress and worshipper of false gods;

To the Earth—it divided itself into enclaves and the unnamed bodies of those who challenged it were lowered into its womb;

To the Sky—cowardly and fainthearted, to save itself from the shrieks and cries it hid itself behind a blue mirage.

Yashodhara asked: 'Shall I tell my story and yours?'

Eve said: 'Your eyes are scarred, so how will they count the wounding arrows that the wind rains down on you?'

Zarrin Taj Qurratul Ain, daughter of Qazwin, said: 'I tried to live like you but the Qajar kings of every age handed over my mystic's raiment to the executioner.'

Danae the goddess of Greek mythology said: 'I was abandoned in a boat in the open sea so I could bear your punishment and my boat went on crashing against unknown islands all my life. I will tell my story.'

Sappho and Anna Akhmatova said: 'Our manuscripts of poetry were snatched away from us; our poetry was deemed shameful for our country—let us tell our tale.'

Blind Safia Bibi said: 'I told your tale without even asking you. The sin of giving birth to a bastard child was mine alone, and the punishment of lashes was also mine to bear.'

Eve burst out: 'Who punished you? Were you alone in this act, absolutely alone?'

In the old chronicles you never find details of incidents, only the judgement and the punishment, to teach a lesson to others.

In Italy Maria of the Valentine family said: 'They say Lake Como emerged from glaciers. Hundreds of villages and thousands of people exist beside its shores. Who knows how many hearts have perished in its waters? I was wed to a 48-year-old prince from Milan. No one thought of my 20-year-old youth. They only saw the wealth and the grand mansion that even today goes by the name of Villa Serbelloni.

'Only Verri could understand the person within me. He was a famous writer. When he gave me the plays of the well-known French playwright de Gouges to translate, I felt as though my veins had learnt to speak. The interaction between words and intellect was also added to the bag of sins and so I enclosed myself within walls of solitude.

'But matters didn't end here. As reparation I had to return the royal curios and wealth one by one. In the palace which bore my name tales of cruelty continued to transpire. This is where Clara and Mussolini were targeted by Valerio's bullets.'

In Sargodha 8-year-old Jacob is locked up in jail. He is an accused. He was writing something on the walls of a mosque. Who knows if he was writing anything? The guardians of the mosque were enraged. They called out to the protectors of the people: 'Jail! Jail Jacob!'

J, Ch, H, G … G for God but M for Man—no, Monkey! Monkey, Mad, Misbehaved, Maniac, Miscreant, Malodorous, Miserable, Malediction, Majesty—our heroes, having caused rivers of blood to flow, address the medal-givers as 'Your Gracious Majesty'.

Monarchs have one wife. Yashodhara too was a wife. So were Sita and Nur Jehan. But Qurratulain Tahira and Umrao Jan Ada were no one's wives. Stories about them were told by many but some remembered them like they do Queen Anne—there it is not only King William's Glorious Revolution that is talked about. In Spain, along with King Ferdinand, Isabella's role in crushing the Arabs is also remembered. Similarly the successes of Catherine of Russia and Theresa of Austria also go into the balance.

Eve! You have changed your name so many times! Sometimes you called yourself Anne Sexton and announced your real birth at the age of 29. Sometimes you were Forough Farrokhzad or Sara Shagufta. And sometimes my mother!

How strange! I am telling the stories of all these people who are no longer alive, in their name. But whenever those who are ostensibly alive will be mentioned it will be as though they are fairy tales. We who even blush at our own reflections in the mirror, how will we bear the burden of being described in words!

Truly, these days when Lawrence is seen as run-of-the-mill and Henry Miller too; when psychological novels are passé; when long, unstructured novels carry no weight and my friends are engaged in freeing the novel and short story from verbiage and the constrictions of technique, then even fact begins to read like fiction.

The problem of today's individual is that he believes neither in nature nor in history. Nor in himself. Who is he? Who will discover his inner being? However, nowhere in the world today is anyone being hanged for his philosophy or drinking a cup of poison.

Galileo, Bacon, Newton, Descartes—the Church censured them all. From Ibn al-Haitham to Ibn-e-Sina all were deemed reprehensible.

For that matter, Bi Amma, Khalida Adeeb Khanum and my mother too were regarded as reprehensible. And no one wrote about the misfortunes of those princesses and mistresses of castles, who were forced to scrub dishes in other people's homes when their circumstances changed, and lived tucked away in attics. Time splits itself into so many stages....

One stage was when Father went from Hapur to Gulavthi to wed my mother. He had been married three times before but the marriages had been short lived. Each wife had gone leaving one or two children behind as keepsakes. The fourth wife—daughter of a Syed, eldest of nine brothers and sisters—came to do the impossible. Having sat in a lap until the age of ten or twelve, she received as her bridal gift stepdaughters to sit in her own lap along with several gardens, scullery maids, and maidservants.

Father was employed in the Court of Ward. He was the manager of Rajghat Naroda. He had left his studies after class eight, while his elder brother had done his matriculation and become a commissioner in the police service.

With regard to Father we had heard it said that he used to write poetry. I had never seen him reading, writing, or listening to poetry. But his coherent writing and well-rounded essays could be seen in his letters, in the Shikasta script that was a paper by itself in the Munshi Fazil examination. For me, as for all my brothers and sisters, the Shikasta script was entirely familiar and easy because it was the script used by our father.

When I saw this style of writing in the *Diwan-e-Hali* in the Islamic collection of the museum of Venice, reading the two pages gave me great pleasure. There also I was thrilled to see Fariduddin Attar's handwritten manuscript *Mantiq al-tayr*, the manuscript of Nizami Ganjvi's book, a handwritten *Shahnama* and Jami's *Yusuf and Zulaikha*. All the handwritten manuscripts including the original *Tarikh al-Tabari*, letters from the time of Ibn Taimur, Abu Hatim's writing on ivory, the Qur'an written in Sicily, the *Kitab al-Nakhl*—all these things were part of my heritage, because my father wrote in the same Shikasta script.

My mother was the eldest daughter of the Maulvi Syed family. All the men in her family were followers of Sir Syed Ahmad Khan. The boys studied at Aligarh; each one was allowed to do his masters in the subject of his choice. After their holidays when the boys went back to the Aligarh hostel special arrangements were made: canisters stuffed with sweet biscuits, sesame seed *laddoos*, carrot *halwa* made with *desi ghee*, *nishasta halwa*, would be sent with them.

With regard to the education of girls it was the same deference to Sir Syed Ahmad Khan: 'Girls should only be taught to read the Qur'an by sight [without comprehension]—and *Behishti Zevar*.' My mother also was only educated to this extent. Did she make a fuss to study like the boys? There is no evidence of this in the attitudes or conversations of the brothers and sisters. Nevertheless, our upbringing and her insistence on the girls' education seem to be a throwback to the wounds suffered by her when she was stopped from studying. There was a great deal of anger in her, and bitterness. This bitterness would invariably poison her sweet temperament.

Mother had first got married at the age of thirteen; the eldest child and much loved, she did not get a loving husband. Rather it became a situation of tit for tat. The henna on her hands had not yet faded when one morning she brought him a cup of milk; finding it hot, he flew into such a rage that he threw the hot milk on her face and pronounced *talaq*. She locked herself in the room and Grandfather had to come and have the door opened and take her home.

This was the same mother who had to cross the bridge of living in a new household with three grownup stepdaughters. Each one had a different mother, each a different temperament. From the very beginning there was no familial affection in the house. And the well of patience invariably ran dry.

Father's not having studied much showed up in his opposition to higher education for the children; to the extent that he refused to give additional money for their education or raise the allowance for the domestic expenses. Our mother would give us one *roti* instead of two. Five brothers and sisters would be made to study around one lantern. She would dish out one piece of meat and gravy with her own hand. When the older brothers and sisters had outgrown their clothes they would be passed on to the younger ones. While she cooked the food, she made us all sit around the stove, teaching us Urdu and sums. Thrusting heavy stones in our tiny hands, she would make us grind whole red chillies, sweep the floor, cook the rotis, but insisted that we should never give up studying.

Dholana was the ancestral home of my mother's family and Gulavthi was where they lived. Grandfather had avoided educating the girls. But he had started a school in Gulavthi: Gohar Girls School. Gohar Bano was the name of my grandfather's mother. Grandfather Fazlur Rahman was himself an advocate whose office was in a completely separate *haveli*. In front of the haveli there were long corridors with rooms where clerks and *qanungos* and those who had come for hearings stayed. My grandmother Amatul Islam taught the Qur'an to the neighbourhood children. When the children were leaving, they would be given baskets filled with fruit from the season's harvest: melons, mangoes, water chestnuts. Fruit was never bought from the market. Despite this prosperity, breakfast would consist of leftover rotis from the night before and tea or home-made beaten curds. Everything was made at home, from vermicelli to *baris*. In addition to lentils and vegetables, beef was cooked in all the homes. However, mutton was bought for those who were sick. But there was no tradition of eating chicken or fish.

Every *dupatta* was dyed at home, every outfit stitched at home, all spices freshly ground. Wheat and rice were cleaned at home by scullery maids. Outfits which had been through several washes were not wasted. It was common to sew patches on men's pyjamas. Turning old sheets into sacks, pillow covers, and tablecloths was considered good housekeeping. Wedding dupattas were turned into linings for quilts and *ghararas* were cut up and used as borders. In spite of all the prosperity it was the custom to put the curry on the roti and eat it. Frugality was in evidence everywhere. After the curry had been taken out, water was never poured into the empty cooking pot: the roti would be used to wipe the inside of the pot first. Matchsticks were rarely used: early in the morning the smaller children like us would be handed the *kurcha* to fetch embers from some other house and this was how the fire would be lit. Even books were bound at home so that after a year they could be used by another child.

Tight pyjamas would be worn in winter but saris and ghararas throughout the year. Most of the women would use Victorian-style hair combs to do up their hair. The little girls were happy so long as they got crimped dupattas glittering with mica—nice new clothes and new shoes were bought only for the two Eids. No wonder then, they would spend the whole night before an Eid looking at the new clothes and thinking: *We'll get to wear them in the morning.*

Our mother never had the time to tell us fairytales. And if some old woman did tell us stories it would be about the coronation of Queen Victoria or the First World War, or about ghosts and spirits. In those days every house had some phantom or the other.

Purdah was customary to such an extent that my maternal grandmother, and for a long time my mother too, never appeared before her sons-in-law. The palanquin would be kept in the *dobari*. A stone would be placed inside, my mother would take her place, and then the palanquin bearers would be summoned. They would set down the palanquin in the same way in the dobari in Grandmother's house; this is how the shortest journey would be covered. We only found out afterwards that the stone was placed in the palanquin in order to hide the real weight of the woman. Holding a flour-dipped hand out for the pulse to be felt and even for little girls to veil themselves upon the entry of the water carrier into the house were part of the social etiquette.

As far as purdah was concerned there wasn't much difference between Hindu and Muslim households. All the Hindu women would go out wrapped in thick *chadors*. No woman's face would appear at the door or window. When palanquins started dying out, white sheets would be tied around *tongas* and this is how Muslim and Hindu women would go out. Between the house and the lane too a passage was made from white sheets held up by the male servants so that the ladies could get into the tongas.

Hapur was my paternal grandfather's district. Father had to go from one town to another in connection with his work; my mother and the kids would accompany him. Our stepsisters would also be with us. Father was very fond of good food, beautiful clothes, and jewellery. He indulged in photography and would also develop films and make enlargements. In line with this obsession he would ask Mother and the children to dress up in all sorts of clothes. From nine-gemmed armlets and seven-stringed necklaces to tinkling anklets, he had taken photographs of Mother in all guises. I had seen her with gold sovereigns and silver coins in my childhood. She used to dispense them by weight. It was during the same period that we had heard that in her father's room there was a pit filled with gold and silver bricks.

Among the coins, in addition to annas and pice, there was also a half-pice coin for which you could get a whole lot of sweets.

Water was brought to the house by water carriers in *mashk*. They would knock on the outer door and announce: 'Veil yourselves! The water carrier is here!' All the women would go into seclusion; the water carrier would fill the jars and leave.

During the early days of the cinema there were silent films. We would go up to the roof and watch silent films being shown on the wall in front, but that too behind Mother's and Father's back.

I also remember the 'marriage' of orchards. Before the first fruit appeared the orchard would be ritually married, and its first harvest distributed among the poor.

Mother and Father were both headstrong. Perhaps in their youth this wilfulness was part of their romantic style. But by the time I became aware conditions had changed; I was the fifth born among their living children. The two eldest sons had died at birth and one in the middle too. I was thus the eighth child and after me there were a brother and a sister who are still living.

Our house was divided into two sections—the male section which was ruled by Father and the other section where everyone stayed was under the command of my mother. When my brother came back from Aligarh he would sleep in the male section. After coming to Bulandshahr, Father left his job, and started operating bus services between Delhi and

Bulandshahr. Now he had an office in Lower Kot near the bus depot. When Mother and Father had had a fight or were upset with each other, we would find out by Father's not coming home from his office. Many days would pass like this, then one day we would see Mother wearing a sari. She would have jasmine flowers in her ears and would be laughing, while Father would be filling earthenware cups with water and placing them on the parapets.

During Father's angry periods Mother would send for a black rooster; a woman would come and take this rooster away and give my mother sugar which had been prayed over. The longer Mother's prayers became, and the more she counted her prayer beads, the less interest Father showed in prayers.

Some other passion was growing inside him, some other flame flickering.

Chapter Two
First Step

The Second World War and the Pakistan Movement arrived at our doorstep at the same time. The war was followed by a period of soaring costs and shortages. Every household got a daily ration of one bottle of kerosene oil. Every household was rationed one thick muslin sari a month. In our home the prayer beads were kept burnished by expedient lies. My younger and older brothers and I would queue up for oil every evening and Mother would keep on reminding us: 'You are not related to each other, or else we will get just one bottle of oil.' Later on we came to know that in Balochistan a lifetime of slavery used to be bartered for just a glass of water. In the Arab world the same oil turned kings into tyrants and a rebel like Princess Sana was sent to the gallows. Camel traders who had started trading in oil invited those with Patriot Missiles, for they too were fond of guarding other people's homes.

Parachutes left over from the Second World War started appearing in the bazaars. To escape from the thick saris Muslim women started opening up the stitching of parachutes and turning them into *shalwars* and ghararas. High-heeled shoes, coats, and sweaters began to be sold in the bazaars and Muslim women would wear these surreptitiously in place of sandals.

It was during this period that Gandhi made the declaration about using the spinning wheel and weaving *khaddar* and many Hindus started wearing only khaddar. The Muslims started their own efforts for a separate country. The same women who had dipped their hand in flour before showing it to the *hakim* and would only go out in a palanquin, started organizing meetings at various places, raising funds, and arousing fervour among the children for a separate and independent nation. We kids who used to play *gulli danda* would pick up the same sticks to carry out processions. '*Ley key rahenge Pakistan/Bat key raheyga Hindustan/Ban key raheyga Pakistan*' (We will get our Pakistan/We will break up Hindustan/We will make our Pakistan). Such slogans would echo from time to time in every lane where the Muslims lived.

Bulandshahr was a city divided into two—the section populated below was called Lower Kot and the one above, Upper Kot. Lower Kot was populated mainly by Hindus—[vegetable] shops were also in Lower Kot. In Upper Kot there were mostly Syeds, revenue officials, and Brahmin Hindus.

At that time there was no bigotry or gulf between Hindus and Muslims. All of us young girls would play on the swings together, chatter across the parapets, and go to school together. It was a missionary school, the teachers mostly Christian missionaries. Hindu, Christian, and Muslim girls would eat together. Muslim girls would study Hindi while Hindu girls would be taught Urdu. In the dance class there was no differentiation between castes. We all learned dancing together. Diwali, Dussehra, and Holi were also celebrated by all. In the same way, Christians and Hindus were among those who came to give greetings for Eid or Baqr Eid. Similarly Muharram was holy for all. *Koonda* feasts would be held in one house and young girls from all the houses would spend the whole night busily preparing food. Whether it was a *majlis* or a *tazia* procession it was treated with the same respect by everyone. On 9 and 10 Muharram all Sunni households would observe the fast. The special *dhania* and *khichra* of Muharram were savoured in all the houses.

In 1946 changes began to appear in the landscape. My older sister appeared for the Middle Vernacular Board Examination. Father had great faith in her intelligence. The results came out: she had come second. Father refused to accept it. He went to Allahabad and had the papers re-examined. A Hindu girl's marks had been fiddled to make her come first. When the fresh results came out my sister stood first. But the pleasure had soured. In everyone's minds there was the same flame burning: this place is closing in on us. This is not our home, not our country. The mangoes from our orchards and swings gave us solace but an unspoken thought had taken root in every courtyard. All the Muslim women had started putting away a handful of flour while kneading dough morning and evening. In every home, one child was given the duty to collect the flour from all the houses, sell it at the shop, and deposit the money at the Muslim League office. When Quaid-i-Azam appealed for donations from the Muslims the women came up with this movement themselves and followed it through. Until Pakistan was made this duty was discharged in every house morning and evening.

Men and women's public meetings were held separately but now joint meetings started to gather steam. Mother would go to the meeting place in her burqa, a child in her lap or clinging to her finger. At home we would trace out the Pakistani flag with candles on sheets of paper or in our copy books. One day a huge procession came out. Who had come? Perhaps Quaid-i-Azam or Liaquat Ali Khan. The same ladies, who only got into their palanquins behind drawn sheets, dressed up their kids and stood waiting at the entrances to their houses with flowers. Time flew by and one evening we saw Father entering the house wearing garlands and carrying a basket of sweets: Pakistan had come into being. Mother ordered: 'First say your prayers of thanksgiving, then eat the sweets!'

It was time for the Isha prayers. We children had gone to sleep. Our happiness was interrupted by bristling soldiers who came in and took Father away. Then we found out that along with my maternal uncle, all the important Muslim leaders in the city had been rounded up. The following day, clutching my tiny shalwar, I was becoming familiar with the jail environment along with my brother. How fate had eased my path! How could I otherwise have assimilated the full horror of what went on in the jails during the Ayub Khan, Yahya Khan, and Ziaul Haq martial laws. In 1970 when I received information about Yusuf's whereabouts—Chakki No. 440, Kot Lakhpat Jail—I knew that each cell is called a *chakki* and this was the number of Yusuf's cell. Greeting Habib Jalib and other friends at the entrance of the jail on the day of his release the thought did not occur that perhaps they would not come this way again. After all, for whom would the prison gates open? In 1970 Yusuf and his father were arrested the same way, at night. Two cars full of army personnel arrived and took him away at four in the morning. In the FIR was written: *The accused has said 'The army is an ass. How can it run a country?'* In this case Yusuf was sentenced to one year's imprisonment. (How this sentence was quashed and the penalty I had to pay for that is for another chapter.) This is why even my children were not afraid when from 1977 to 1979 I was under CID surveillance. One motorcycle would be in front of me and one jeep behind me. All this outspoken loudmouth was doing was reciting poetry to vent her anger at martial law. What else could one do? Every unlawful action and every unimaginable tyranny was going on in front of us like a nightmare from which there is no escape. But this period was an eye opener in another way as well. There were many friends who apologized for not coming to visit at the house or in the office, on the pretext that car numbers were being noted down, and names and addresses too. My own visits to other people's homes declined as I didn't want to see any friend being embarrassed. But hats off to my kids and neighbours. The pride with which they encouraged me and the ways in which they tricked the CID resulted in no little amusement. What could the poor wretches do? They were just following orders. When my children took food out to them they would be even more ashamed and when their duty was over and those who had to go to the gallows were hung what did it achieve! What happened to people everywhere!

In Bosnia people were forced to eating their own excreta. Their women were raped in front of them. In Somalia and Ghana famine-struck people were reduced to eating the hides of camels. In Kashmir the houses became empty; there are only women and children but they don't weep and wail. The women of Palestine and Kashmir who would not even utter a 'yes' at the time of their marriage, now have guns in their hands. They wrap the shrouds over their children themselves—my eyes become misty.... Peace, harmony, tranquillity, national security...at what a price, what a heavy price. In the scale of the big countries we have no value. The whorehouses of the capitalistic system attack these days in the name of war for human liberties....

The period from the founding of Pakistan and leading up to Father's release was one of strange restlessness. It had already been decided that we would go to Pakistan but when and how were still unknown. During that period every night was a night of torment. Every night there would be rumours—today armed posses from such and such village will attack and carry off the girls. All night long Muslim boys would stand guard with sticks on the rooftops and the whole night women would be counting their prayer beads.

Aligarh was still identified with Muslim boys and girls. The boys' uniform was black *sherwani* with tight *pajamas* and for the girls ghararas made of *latha* cloth, and black burqas. In our eyes, the girls who studied at Aligarh led a charmed life. We used to dream that we would grow up to live and study like them in Aligarh. This dream was in tatters before our eyes. A huge crowd had gathered. All the women were standing in shock, their eyes red like embers. The girl who was the darling of the whole city and studied at Aligarh had been kidnapped. God knows through how many jungles she had wandered, bleeding from everywhere. Now she lay unconscious. Sympathy there was, but all kinds of phrases were being bandied about and every mother was gathering her offspring to her bosom.

It was during this period that I began to shriek in my sleep at night. Mother would blow prayers over me; she would read the Ayat al-Kursi, walk with me in her lap until the morning's *azaan* sounded.

How believable are the shrieks uttered in dreams when shrieks uttered in the full light of day are taken to be dreams? It all happened in daylight; in broad daylight the announcement was made. I remember it like I do every wound. I had been to Bengal several times before. I had hosted many Bengali poets, friends, and women's groups. But this was a strange invitation—there was no host, nor guest. This was in September 1971. I was sent on an official visit to Bengal to write a booklet in favour of the government hoodlums [Al Shams and Al Badr] who were fighting against the Bengalis. I went immediately. You can't feel burning or pain unless you jump into the fire. There was a camp beside the Burhi Ganga River full of women. Can I really call them women? Scrawny girls barely thirteen to fifteen years old, whose breasts had not yet emerged but whose bellies indicated that they were six or seven months pregnant. Where were their families? They had been killed under cover of night as conspirators and traitors. To sully their bloodline the women had been ravished. Homeless and unprotected, they sat with head bowed, parched lips, and dry eyes in Burhi Ganga's lap.

I had heard on BBC that in order to get the Iqbal Hall, one of the hostels for Dhaka University students, vacated, all the boys had been killed. After much searching I arrived at Iqbal Hall. It was being whitewashed from outside. When I entered, scorched clothes and the smell of gunpowder bore witness to the brutality.

Some of my friends seeing my madcap actions and the fuss that I was making put me on a plane right away. My report was censured at the official level. All my friends and I who had spoken out on behalf of the Bengalis were regarded as traitors and unpatriotic. I could not say anything because the day the announcement came, the 5 o'clock evening news had only this to say: 'The armies of both the sides have laid down their arms by mutual agreement.'

When I left my house to condole with likeminded friends and to mourn with them, I let out an uncontrollable shriek at the scene before me. It was unbelievable, but real: people were laughing; unconcerned; eating ice cream. For six months afterwards I couldn't speak. No doctor could understand the reason for it.

Some years later I went to India. There, on a street hoarding, was the historic photograph of General Arora and General Niazi, which is framed and occupies a whole wall in the Dhaka museum. Below the hoarding was written: 'The victor's uniforms are made of cloth manufactured by our firm.' And in the Dhaka National Liberation Museum, below the photograph is the caption: 'At last Bangladesh is free. The Pakistani army chief is laying down his arms.'

In Dhaka the National Liberation Museum was spread over a whole floor, and photographic, journalistic, and literary documentation of the struggle of the Bengalis against the Pakistan army was preserved there. In one corner there was a table on which was written: 'The historic table on which the Pakistani army signed the surrender document.' The officials of the Pakistani High Commission warned me repeatedly: 'Don't go to see that museum. You will feel bad.' I said to myself: '*Khoon key dhabbay dhulenge kitni barsaaton key bad*'[1] (How many monsoons will it take to wash away these bloodstains). To understand this line I will have to visit this killing field.

The mother of four daughters was clueless about her own future and that of her husband. She was not a passenger on any departing train, nor was she waiting for the arrival of one! *Clickety-clack*! At last in September 1949 a Hindu friend of Father's made a booking on a train. After his release Father had managed to cross the border with the help of his Hindu friends. On the other hand, restrictions had been imposed on the arrival of Mohajirs on the border. How would we go?

Once again the expedient lie came to our aid. Government servants were still allowed to send for their families. A cousin declared us as his family and arranged to invite us. Father's friend made the arrangements to send us but had to bring us back from the platform. All those who were present there were imploring: 'Go back! Save the girls!' In the train that had left the night before all the young men had been shot one by one while the girls had been carried off—once again we were neither passengers on a departing train nor waiting for an approaching one.

The decision was made: abandon the household goods, sell the jewellery, get tickets on the Dakota plane and look to the safety of the children. Once again the expedient lie came in handy—I had been made to wear a burqa from the age of seven but with a burqa you needed a full ticket, whereas children until the age of twelve only needed half a ticket. The burqa was whisked off and all of us arrived at Lahore airport from Delhi.

I had been jotting down some names throughout the journey—Adha Pakaji—the fat Brahmin teacher who taught us Hindi. Always in a white muslin sari, with covered head and a shining face. Whenever a girl poked her hand or face out through the curtains of the tonga, she immediately gave her a slap. Whenever I got good marks in Hindi she gave me a kiss. Miss Ghosh, the English teacher who mischievously caught the thread which had been passed through my newly-pierced nose and ears and said: 'Repeat after me. This is Mother's punishment for failing in English!' The hurt, both from the thread being pulled and the failure, would bring tears to my eyes. To punish myself I cut off the threads from my ears and nose. I never wore jewellery. But does closing the holes in one's ears and nose stop that vortex of voices?

And that *shamshan ghat* on the way to school, where the Hindus would cremate their dead, where we had been forbidden to stop, where there was always a thin line of smoke which swims in the sockets of my eyes even today.... After Yusuf died whenever I went to the graveyard, that shamshan ghat would confront me. Some images keep enlarging over time.

NOTE

1. The fourth line in Faiz Ahmed Faiz's poem, *Dhaka se wapsi par* (On returning from Dhaka), written after a visit to Bangladesh after its independence.

Chapter Three
First Prostration

On Fridays whenever I have to pass through Lahore's Mall Road, I slow down my car near Masjid-e-Shuhada. Sometimes I stand near the footpath. Words spew out from the microphone in a terrifying voice. I move to a different street and park my car at Nila Gumbad. Here too I get no relief. I stand near the stairs of the Shahi Masjid; the cheap perfume from the *burqa*-clad women brushing past clogs up my nose. I block my ears.

I think about the young and old in my family, who go to say their prayers with great humility and fear of God; they fast; they offer their five daily prayers; they open the *Behishti Zevar*, read its verses and offer the sacrifice; the women read the Milad-e-Akbar; they pray for blessings which, after passing through hundreds of thousands of angels and *imams*, only get to some poor soul with difficulty. All of them, my own people, having listened to the ravings of the *maulvi* in the form of the *khutba*, in their own neighbourhoods, return home like sheep and are back again in the mosque the following week.

We had all finished the Qur'an by the age of seven. Mother would teach us herself; breakfast would only be served after we had recited a chapter. I would feel so hungry that several times I tried to skip a page or two, but even though Mother would be busy cooking the rotis and getting my other brothers and sisters ready for school, she would turn on me like a shot: 'What did you do wrong? Read it correctly.' Grumbling in anger and irritation, I would turn back to the missed page under Mother's piercing gaze. My blood would boil and I would scream: 'I am hungry!' One slap. My head would spin and after this the pages dampening with tears and the recitation in a voice choked with hiccups was all that the chapter was worth.

It was forbidden to read the Qur'an with comprehension on the basis that doing so negated the reward. Those who were illiterate were told: 'You just run your fingers along the lines of the verses; you will get the same rewards as in reading the Qur'an.' Every religious obligation had to be fulfilled on Mother's orders like Allah's commandments. Even in the depths of summer all the children would observe the fast and walk to school. The funny thing was that the warnings themselves would show us the way to mischief. We were ordered: 'Don't even think of drinking water surreptitiously in the bathroom. Allah is watching.' When I couldn't bear the thirst I would go to the bathroom and say: 'Oh, Allah you can see how thirsty I am. Look, I am drinking water.' I don't know if Allah likes my addressing him directly or not. But it's been a habit my whole life that in moments of helplessness I address Allah directly and look for an answer. But Allah has also shown me a time when people would display a prayer mat and *lota* prominently in their room just for show; when the Public Service Commission while testing doctors would ask: 'Recite the Namaz-e-Janaza'; when it asked professors of Urdu: 'Recite the Dua-e-Qunoot'; when it asked teachers of geography: 'Recite the third Kalima'; and ordered scientists: 'Say, the combination of hydrogen and oxygen creates water by the grace of God.'

During the days of poverty and helplessness that followed our coming to Pakistan, there were strange liberties and constraints. Before shifting to other houses there were many families living together in one house like sheep in a pen. There were restrictions on talking to male cousins of the same age. You couldn't stand at the window looking at the clothes on the mannequins in the showcases of the shops in Anarkali bazaar. There were no books to read; only the Qur'an. I had made reading the Qur'an day and night, reading its meaning and even the Tahajjud prayers, a part of my daily routine. Once again everyone became cross. 'She's gone mad! Prayers and ablutions all the time! It's not good to read the Qur'an at noon or when day and night meet. It's not good to eat and drink at that time either... stop it!'

I remember when, having got fed up of my antics, Mother sent me to a woman to finish reading the Qur'an. Her house was some distance away at the corner of a lane. This woman would first have me wash the dishes or sweep the floor. She would get me to knead the dough and say: 'Hazrat Bibi Fatima would do all her work herself! If you adopt the same habits you will also have a life of ease.' With the chapter open in front of me, I would start grumbling: 'What a nuisance! At home Mother gets us to grind the spices which burn our hands. And Bua makes me sweep the floor and my crimped dupatta gets dirty.' This went on every day. I would grumble more and read less.

One evening the neighbourhood girls were returning home together after reading the Qur'an. Our lane was a cul-de-sac and we would all play hide and seek. Satisfied that no outsider could enter, the families were happy to let the girls play together. All of a sudden the girl who was 'it' shrieked 'Ooooeee! What's this?' The others all turned around. The elderly gentleman from the corner house on the right was going back in hastily tying his *kamarband*. The girls all started badgering the one who had been 'it'. 'What happened? Tell us. What did he do? Did the old man say something?' And the girl who was 'it'—me—could only stare straight ahead, with pointing finger, dumbstruck, lips trembling, drenched in sweat. The old crones from some of the houses, understanding the delicacy of the situation and figuring it out without asking for details, pushed the girls into their respective houses. After that my going to the old lady's house was stopped.

At the time I was offering Tahajjud prayers and *jalali wazifas* I was around ten years old. I didn't feel frightened in the least waking up at 2 a.m. and sitting on the prayer mat after performing the ablution. It was summer. Everyone was sleeping on the rooftop. I was on the prayer mat. A strange thing happened—it was as if a finger had passed right through me like a shadow. My mouth became bitter; once more my body was drenched in sweat. I turned towards Mother's bed but she wasn't there. I turned towards Father's bed; his bed was empty too. I looked towards the terrace below; the same shadow was standing on a prayer mat. In rage I picked up my mat and threw it down. I did not understand then and I don't now. I did not understand *Thanda Gosht*[1] either and when I took the book to my brother asking: 'What is there in it over which the lawsuit is going on? I have read it several times but I can't get it.' Thwack! I got a slap on my face and the book was snatched out of my hand. So many books snatched out of one's hands! In childhood it was family members, and in adulthood the government. But why fret. Just look at your history. The burning of books on the crossroads are pages from your own heritage. The banning of books has happened during your own time. There is no need to go into the history of *fatwas*. At every step, in every country, Muslims are the target of stoning.

When blind Safia Bibi declared: 'I have been raped. I am pregnant. I don't know the name of the rapist,' she got a slap on the face from the Shariah Court. Her sentence was 20 lashes and 14 years' imprisonment. On hearing the decision she too was drenched in sweat. Neither Earth nor Sky can believe it, but it did happen in Pakistan. During the 14 years from 1979 to 1993, husbands sent their wives to jail on allegations of Zina, so they could marry a second time without hindrance. Brothers accused sisters of Zina, and in gobbling up their inheritance felt their manhood vindicated. Fathers got their daughters accused of Zina to prevent them from marrying of their own will so that they could lay their hands on the dowry which would make their own lives comfortable.

All this is not being written by a Wolpert or Khushwant Singh who could be branded a bigot or a liar. If lawyers like Hina Jilani, Asma Jahangir, Rashida Patel, Shaheen Sardar Ali and Fakhrunnisa had not been there perhaps these facts, like princesses, would also have been sealed up within walls.

People quote examples from Pharaoh's time. That is held to be the pre-Islamic period. But the promulgators of Islam and the Shariah Courts have even alleged that the 13-year-old Balochi girl who accused her father of rape was doing it on the instigation of her maternal uncle who wanted to grab her share of the property.[2] I am watching—I am listening.

Then a time came when fathers began to compete in getting cases filed involving Zina *with* their daughters. This is not a tale from Pharaoh's time. These are real-life incidents that took place in 1993 in the rural areas of the glorious land of Pakistan. For the sake of money fathers accepted this shame and our illustrious sons showed it on television—a slap on the faces of all women.

Childhood memories are less of fairytales or stories of princesses from *Alif Laila* (*The Thousand and One Nights*) and more of the scourges of fear. It's a different matter that youth and old age had to go through the same fire and turn into ash.

Fear of the hereafter was drummed into me with the first breath of consciousness. If you played with dolls, at once a shout: 'Stop it or you'll have to bring them to life on the Day of Judgement!' If you made two plaits, then a curse: 'On the Day of Judgement two snakes will be tied to your head!' If you didn't wear bangles, a rebuke: 'Allah does not accept the prayers of a woman who doesn't wear bangles. On the Day of Judgement you'll be taken to task!' If you climbed up to the rooftop, a hue and cry: '*Ai hai*! A demon will get you! *Ai hai*! What a long thick plait. A djinn will get after you! Go, cover your head! Get down or on the Day of Judgement you'll have to explain yourself in front of Allah!'

Sometimes I would hold up reeds like *alams* and beat my chest like Imam Hussain's mourners and read *marsiyas*. The moment Mother saw me she would pull me by my plaits: 'Wretch! Bringing a bad name to a Syed household. Beating your chest. On Judgement Day Allah will strike *your* chest!'

'*Ai hai*! Marrying of her own accord! The Shariah forbids it. I won't forgive her. I will never look at her face again!' For several years Mother did not see my face and when she did she did not take me into her arms and kiss me. A limp hand was placed on my head. The warmth of the womb goes deep inside; it does not hide its fire.

'*Ai hai*! She is going back to work just 15 days after her husband's death. She is not even completing the *iddat*! God forgive us. What have we come to?'

Yes, staying inside your house, bent over the stove the whole day, slaving away for the family, that's the *iddat* of the Shariah. Leaving that, to drown your loneliness in files, is to prepare your bed in Hell.

'Woman is inferior...otherwise she would have been God, she would have been a prophet, she would have been equal to man....This is why woman can't be head of state.' Who is saying this...who is giving this judgement? All those who were rejected by the masses. Who the masses did not vote for, who they did not hold capable of being their representatives. They only dare to start using the shield of religion the day after the masses give their verdict against them. They are men...they are God... because they have always portrayed God as male. In childhood, whenever God's majesty was talked about, I would imagine Him sitting in the sky like a king. No one explained why prayers and protection are only sought for while looking up towards the sky when, if He is there, then He is closer to you than your jugular vein. If He is there, and even a leaf cannot flutter without His orders, then a woman's becoming prime minister, not once but twice, is proof of some wisdom, some message! A friend from London says: 'Woman is mother, she procreates. You call the creator God but deny the equality of women.' Colleagues agitated to ban her book and then to have her kicked out of the department. My book was also banned on the pretext of religious morality. In 1983 I was in America and learnt about the ban from the American press. What had I done? Only translated Simone de Beauvoir's *The Second Sex*. The English edition had not been banned. They said the Urdu translation was a base attempt to publicize immoral issues with regard to the female body. Therefore, five notices were published in the newspapers, announcing the censorship separately for each province and for the whole country.

I had presented the body of a blossoming woman with its psychological ramifications. So, okay, perhaps it titillated the clerks who read it. But what was there in Ikramullah's book *Gurg-e-shab* or in Fakhar Zaman's book: *Ik Maray Banday di Kahani*?

Censoring words through clerks continued for ten years during which they even went so far as to censor Qur'anic verses. Allama Iqbal's '*Ya tera gareban chaak ya daaman-e-yazdan chak*' was not allowed to be broadcast on radio or television. No man could touch a woman on television. They could not sit on a bed together. This is not about something happening in the sixteenth century; it is to do with people who were trumpeting: 'We want to enter into the twenty-first century.'

All this reminds me of the stories of the Hungarian short-story writer Géza Csáth. His view is that mother and whore—in both garbs—woman is reprehensible because these relationships are just guises to grab man's wealth and the fruit of his labour. In his eyes only the dream woman is good, because she doesn't make any demands.

What can I do? Those who have a monopoly on religion don't allow me to obtain the books of writers like Khayyam, Ghori, Amichai, and Karmi. In Bellagio where I am at present, every day we eat the fruits that grow here; we drink the water from the stream that flows in front. But even though I feel refreshed by its bracing wind I cannot say that it is heaven.

On the basis of religion an 80-year-old woman like Shah Bano in Hyderabad Deccan had to return the rights granted to her by the court. Having delegated the right to men to marry four wives, society feels satisfied.

A Lebanese friend asked me, 'Have you read Al-Khansa's poetry?' I replied, 'Yes, as much as was available.' He asked, 'And the poetry of the pre-Islamic age?' I replied, 'I don't know anything about it.' The Lebanese friend said, 'That was the age of true knowledge and true poetry. That's the poetry we were taught in school.'

While to us, in the name of religion, *Behishti Zevar*, *Pakki Roti* and *Kamasutra* were permissible. But the door to knowledge slammed shut! The poetry of the pre-Islamic age unacceptable! *Inni kunto min az zaalimeen* (Truly, I was among the tyrants).

NOTES

1. A collection of short stories by Saadat Hasan Manto. It includes the short story *Thanda Gosht* (Cold Meat), regarded as obscene. On account of this story Manto faced prosecution
2. Report of the Shariah Court.

Chapter Four
First Idol

Just as you get used to slipping in and out of an old pair of shoes without looking, in the same way going up and down the ladders of relationships does not make you breathless. After all, it's only trying to capture real, live moments that takes your breath away.

My sign is Gemini; its symbol is two faces. Light and shade in Gemini, they say. Seven women come alive to narrate this tale of mine; turn by turn they will change their guise. Sometimes it will be Mahlaqa, sometimes Laila, Zarrin Taj, or Meera Bai. There will also be tales of princesses like Yashodhara and Sana. There is of course Eve because the amazing talisman which makes the known unknown and renders the conscious into the unconscious is bent on turning the pen into a sword.

But in this narrative the story of homelessness and migration is yet to come. The father who moved from jail to Pakistan considered it immoral to file a claim and so we lived under other people's roofs, sometimes in the lanes of Garhi Shahu, sometimes Santnagar, sometimes Krishannagar.

The fruitless search for a house continued till 1953 when we shifted to Mohammadnagar, a locality in Garhi Shahu. It was a newly-settled area. The girls in all the houses were young. How they would laugh. They would peep out from behind the *chiks* and, poking their legs half out of the chiks, would allow the colour of their feet to hint at the beauty of their faces. Four years after coming to Pakistan this was the first time it felt like home. It was difficult to get admission into school. I had come after completing class eight and there was no way I could get directly into class nine. The teachers took a test. Even getting the top marks could not solve the problem of admission. It was the same situation in private schools. But finally, after God knows what exertions, I got admission into class nine. It was during this period that I became interested in writing for the newspapers. Became interested also in English and in reading books in English. I subscribed to the English newspaper with my own pocket money because the others read the Urdu newspaper and in the English newspaper, every week, the children's page would carry a story or essay by me. It was also during this period that the newspapers started the pen-pal's column. I also wrote in. The result: a deluge! Every day 50 or 60 letters and Mother would have a fit. 'How did she have the guts? Getting letters from bloody men!'

But when she saw that the sisters and brothers were all enjoying it and the whole thing was ending up as a joke she cooled down a bit. (The same deluge of mail was there too after Yusuf's death. Here, even if it's a public hanging, people flock with their tiffin carriers to see the show.) When they saw Mother's rage abating, the interest of the other brothers and sisters grew. One gentleman had written twice in the same letter that he wanted to meet me, and they replied to him on my behalf that I was also dying to meet him. A few days later dressed in a *bosky* shalwar and *kamiz*, clutching an armful of presents, he descended from a tonga. Then all hell broke loose! Everyone was thunderstruck. Because all the brothers and sisters were complicit in the prank, I escaped being clobbered to bits. Nevertheless, seeing the seriousness of the individual and the amount of presents he had brought, everyone was worried at the thought of having to reciprocate.

When he saw the true situation, that the lady in question was only 13 years old, that she studied in class nine, that she had only written in the pen-pal's column for fun, even then he was not disheartened and went off saying that he was prepared to wait for many years. Subsequently he wrote countless letters but they were all objects of ridicule and laughter. When this story leaked out into the neighbourhood, it triggered romantic and competitive feelings among the boys of my own age. Was it necessary after all that Heer's Ranjha should come all the way from Takht Hazara? Then what happened? On the rooftops, instead of flying kites, boys would drop them on to the other roofs when they saw girls there. A note would be scrawled on the kite or on a paper attached to it: 'Show me your face.' Or sometimes 'Let's meet.' And the sign of the immature lover: 'Give me something to identify you with and take something of mine.' Here a handkerchief embroidered with pink roses would be attached. The wicked goings on on the rooftop were unknown to all. When I would go to school, despite being in a burqa, they would follow me from the bus stop to the school. I was fed up. So I took advice from some friends and turned to a teacher; then the boys were sorted out.

The boys may have been sorted out but the teacher lost her head. Now she started coming to leave me to the house thinking that I was still afraid. Everyone at home was convinced of her affection and full of praises but I was terrified that all the other teachers would make fun of me—as the teacher's pet. She was the teacher of Persian. I knew the *Gulistan* and *Bustan* in Persian by heart—she just had to say one word and I would tell the whole story—she would mention a title and I would repeat the narrative. Seeing my abilities she asked class nine to write an essay in Persian in the examination. At that time the girls were only learning to form sentences. They were petrified at having to do an essay, while I was done with it in minutes. My essay created quite a stir and class ten was also shown a copy of my paper. In the annual exam, however, I would not get high marks. Girls like me who gave references from outside reading would get low marks on the basis that we had gone beyond the requirements. A price has to be paid for individuality whether it is in life, learning, or employment.

I had to pay a price for my knowledge of Persian as well. One day the teacher told my mother: 'I want to take her home.'

I dissuaded her, in fact, I refused to go, at which Mother said harshly: 'You don't even accept love; the teacher loves you so much but like the *urad* flour you are becoming stiffer and stiffer.'

What could I do? I went. It was the beginning of winter and the fashion was to drape a shawl over the lower burqa. I did so and went to Mughalpura.

The teacher must have alerted them at the house already, because the white embroidered sheet especially reserved for guests was laid out on the bed, still with its creases. There were also matching flowered pillowcases. The floor had been newly washed. The stove was hot. As soon as we arrived in the room, and before any conversation could begin, a plate of ready-peeled boiled eggs arrived. Seating me beside her she stuffed an egg into my mouth and sidling up really close said: 'Go on, eat!'

God knows why the laughter of all the teachers and girls started echoing in my head. With the egg half in and half out of my mouth I said 'I...bathroom...'

At once I was shown the way to the bathroom. The privy seat made of bricks was enough to allow me to stand and breathe freely. When I returned, halwa, tea, and biscuits had been tastefully arranged on the table. The problem was that there was only one bed in the room; not even a chair. You had to sit on the bed. I still hadn't grasped the situation clearly because despite having read Manto's story *Thanda Gosht*, several times, I hadn't understood it. I couldn't even ask anyone as to what it really meant. But I had read—surreptitiously and over and over again—in the novels of M. Aslam, Qaisi Rampuri and others about the assignations of the hero and heroine and their wedding night. This would be followed by a long sigh and a quick change in mood as I looked around to see if anyone had been watching.

Anyway, all those stories began to come alive as I felt the teacher's hand on my forehead and mouth. With a push I was on the bed and in her embrace, but when she let go of me for a moment to straighten the second pillow, I put my hands together and started crying and imploring: 'Please forgive me! Let me go home.'

Her mother came in and I picked up my burqa and rushed out. I kept running until I reached the house. Everyone was astonished to see the pallor of my face. But upon my explaining that today the Persian lesson had been extra difficult they all turned their attention to more important things.

Stories of love affairs in the school between the girls and the teachers were commonplace. We used to think that those who didn't want to study would get entangled in such nonsense. But we certainly saw how these girls deliberately stood on the path that the teachers had to cross. Giving them embroidered handkerchiefs, shawls, pillow covers, and knitted sweaters; plucking a flower, even if only from the school gardens and leaving it in the teachers' room first thing in the morning so that she could put it in her hair. Most of these girls were studying just for fun. But we, who were serious students, were perhaps also cowards. Although we also wanted something to happen, we had settled for the romance of the written word and the literary landscape.

During this period marriage with an army man seemed very romantic. When the girls were together they would be chattering about their cousins in the army—conversations, secret notes, letters. Although it would all seem like a figment of their imagination, I would regret my own lack of resources in not having a cousin in the army so I could also concoct an imaginary lover. This regret is still with me otherwise I too would have been able to achieve promotions and status without any effort. But was it necessary that there should, in fact, be a cousin? When the mind can create an entire panorama it could also have manufactured a cousin. But if the practice of not losing a grip on reality has started from childhood, then breadth of vision does not manifest itself without depth of feeling.

I asked permission from my family to appear for my matriculation exams because the school had reserved a large room where the studious girls could stay day and night. I said I would stay there. My demand was fulfilled. I stayed there to study but I learnt something else: if the headmistress and the second mistress were in the room we were not allowed to enter it. Now our preparations were put aside in order to find out what the two were up to on one bed. I immediately thought of 'Miss'. But I couldn't confide in anyone else. Late at night we were studying when we heard the noise of laughter and whispering—Thump! Thump! (*Moan*)…Stop…wait! We looked at each other astonished and embarrassed. We couldn't even go home, having come to study. The month which should have been spent in serious preparations was seriously wasted. For me it was particularly unpleasant, having escaped from the experience before.

After I had appeared for the exam I got interested in singing. I knew all the film songs already; I knew the name of the film and the singer by heart. In every gathering I would be asked to sing and I would sing in my thin reedy voice. I knew that some people were laughing. But I would reason that the same thing had happened with the great singers too. I knew all the words so I thought singing was no big deal. But sadly, my singing and my devotion to it were cast aside by my result: I had got First Division with good marks. When I talked about entering college I was told: 'Are you mad? Has anyone from your family studied further? Haven't you got your answer? Why are you then insisting?'

I said: 'But I have got a scholarship.'

The reply: Your older sister also got one but we didn't let her study.'

I couldn't understand how the same mother who had been such a firebrand in front of her own father, was now being so retrogressive in front of us. The same mother who—the moment she had come to Pakistan—had taken the whole family to Islamia College to listen to the address of Liaquat Ali Khan. The same mother who had gone to Aligarh to see my brother get his degree when Sarojini Naidu was the Vice Chancellor (my ears still echo with the voice of Sarojini Naidu). The same mother who allowed us sisters to wear short burqas when the tradition in UP was to wear them down to the feet. After coming to Pakistan the new fashion we had learnt was to wear burqas which came to just below the knees. Some girls would wear burqas that covered their arms and there would be so many pleats that the figure could be clearly made out. Afterwards we found out that these special burqas were worn by Qadianis and we came to understand a little of Lahore, the city which was rocked by the Qadiani controversy in 1953.

Apart from Mother there was no one who could be appealed to. The older sisters were in a state of stupor already. For one it had been six years since she had done her matriculation and for the other eight years. They were not getting married, nor were they going any further. The reason for not getting married was that after coming to Pakistan the search was on for such sons of Syeds who were decent to the extent of being idiots. Boys who smoked cigarettes, wore suits, and allowed their mothers and sisters to go about without the burqa were regarded as 'fast'. They could not marry the sisters. Both Mother and Father had vowed not to have any marriages within the family. So for the sisters it was like a fun fair—cooking, housework, visiting, embroidery, knitting, reading, or listening to dramas on the radio.

On Saturdays at 8:30 p.m. there would be a radio drama. The whole house, rather, the whole neighbourhood, would listen to the drama together without fail. In the morning at 6:30 Radio Ceylon would broadcast old film songs and requests. In the evening was the weekly programme Binaca Geet Mala and it was a must to remember which song had been at the top the week before and which one had been continuously at the top of the charts for how many weeks. It was during this period also that the voices of Mohni Hameed and Begum Haseeb Malik were the life of the radio.

Mohni Hameed's laugh and her voice were a source of envy. After some days we found out that she lived in our own neighbourhood. Being a fan of the radio, Mother allowed her to be asked to the house. She was invited to come for a meal. She asked Mother to make her a gharara and Mother made her one. Hearing my voice she sent me a contract for taking part in programmes on the radio. All hell broke loose! Mother's tears turned the house upside down. How could the voice of a Syed girl echo throughout the world! God forbid! The voices of the adolescent girls of this house don't even go as far as the reception hall. Where did this celebrity come from?

It may have been a disgrace. But in my place my younger sister was given permission to take part in the children's programme. My younger brother and sister would go to the children's programme and I would send jokes, stories, and riddles through them and take consolation from the fact that my work was being broadcast on the radio.

Despite my insistence my college entrance was shelved. All my protests were to no avail. Six months passed. I was cross with the whole house, refusing to go to functions, to smile or talk. Still no permission to enter college. I appealed to my brother who was in Canada. The other brother had also started part-time work. I also implored him. In the end it was decided 'You will be allowed to enter next year. And your older sister will also go with you. Just sit out this year.'

Now the problem was to pass the time. This has been a problem for me all my life. I can't hang about doing nothing. In the mornings every day we would go to the hospital. There would only be one or two who were sick—and what a sickness! One had pimples on her face, another had period pains. What kind of illnesses were those? But there could be no objection to going to the hospital. We would get there walking. Why would we go there? One reason was that it helped to pass the time. We would observe the new doctors' clothes, new fashions, blush at the women's conversations and, seeing the men stare and laugh, we too would be merry all the way home. On returning home there would be *besani* roti, mango or turnip pickle, or mango chutney for lunch. On rainy days rotis stuffed with lentils, *shami kebabs* and an assortment of chutneys would be made.

We were not allowed to watch films. But Father bought tickets for *Pukar*, his favourite film, and took us to see it and Mother took us to see *Zeenat*. Sometimes after much begging and pleading we would be allowed to see an English film on the pretext that it was based on a course book. That was how we went to see films.

What does it mean 'we'? I didn't write 'us brothers and sisters'. Despite the bad blood of today, we still have a lot of affection for each other but it was not part of our upbringing to declare boundless love. We were certainly brothers and sisters who would study around one table with a single lantern; were brought up under one roof. But the kind of siblings who shower each other with love and affection and make sacrifices for each other are only found in films. There is a fine line between competitiveness and envy. To take every opportunity to present another's good point or success like a complaint allows us to believe in our own existence.

After a certain age sisters can fit into each other's clothes. I was the only one who would slip on the completely new clothes of my sisters, slip out from another door and go off to college. Naturally this infuriated everyone—from Mother to all the sisters. They would complain no end and hide their clothes. Mother's beautiful silk and muslin saris which were wearing out along the creases from being kept folded so long, these too I would take out from the boxes and wear.

It is possible that wearing each other's clothes was so annoying because we would make our clothes from the money saved from Eidee, prizes, or pocket money. Otherwise we would only get white shalwar and kamiz to wear to school and college—one shalwar which we would wear in college regularly for seven days. We would be so careful that we would only sit on the grass on Saturdays. Otherwise for six days the fear of soiling the shalwar would not allow us to sit on the grass.

Wealth had not begun to affect colleges as yet. We would all buy one *samosa* each or take out the *aloo parathas* or rotis brought from home, and eat lunch together. The canteen was flourishing under the patronage of the hostel girls or the rich girls. There was a strange atmosphere as far as studies went.

We would see the Urdu lecturer delivering her lecture after reading poetry guides published in Urdu Bazaar in the teachers' room. In the same way the geography and economics teachers had notes dating back to several years before the independence of Pakistan. They would be repeating those constantly.

Studying is to a certain extent a personal endeavour. The real thing is the environment, the relationship between teacher and student, tutorials, pedagogy. With admission into college, the season of debates and *mushairas* also started. I put down my name for debates. But there was no question of doing so for mushairas: to remember verses was one thing, to write verses was altogether different. The thought hadn't even entered my head that I could compose verse. The teacher knew of my interest in Urdu and the store of verses I had memorized. I knew by heart verses from *Bang-e-Dira, Bal-e-Gibril, Diwan-e-Ghalib* and the ones read in mushairas. I had notebooks filled with my favourite verses. I had written down entire mushairas broadcast on the radio. But I had never thought of composing verse.

This was the time when one poetess had recited her work in a mushaira at the University Hall and people had broken down the chairs and glass door panes. The mushaira had been mentioned in the papers, radio, and magazines, in a derisive way. Questions were asked as to who had written the verses for her. My young mind would erupt in anger on hearing those questions. I still remember her—a small, dark girl, like me, without looks (I didn't say bad looking), about whom they would all say: 'Don't look at her—just listen to her voice! What amazing modulation! What accomplished verses! See, she has even left Hafeez and Josh far behind. Surely it's the doing of some teacher.'

I always had the habit of muttering when I was angry. At home also I would protest at the quips of my brothers. Why couldn't a woman compose verse? I couldn't display my anger in front of anyone. But everywhere on my own I would stand up for her. During this time one of the magazines issued a supplement on celebrities with essays on the personalities of women short-story writers. I used to read this magazine over and over again. After coming across one account of writing while lying on the stomach, face down, chewing betel nut, I too would try to read my course books lying face down. Who would bring all this literature for me at the time? It was all the doing of a man who I regarded as a brother. He loved to write poetry. Seeing my interest in reading poetry and literature he gave me a present. In those days the annual subscription for literary magazines was 12 rupees, which was a big sum as we only got four annas for pocket money every month. He sent me works by A. Hameed, Manto, Krishan Chandar, Ismat Chughtai and the poetry of Shelley, Keats, and Browning. If I asked him about English novels he would say: 'You are too young.'

So I started bringing English books from the school and subsequently college libraries. Whenever anyone saw a novel in my hands there would be a hue and cry. So then I changed my routine of reading books. In the early part of the evening the other brothers and sisters would be studying. I would go off to sleep and at 4 o'clock in the morning when everyone would be sleeping I would calmly be reading fiction and novels along with my course books. It was during this time that I read books like *War and Peace, Anna Karenina* and *And*

Quiet Flows the Don. In childhood I had read Deputy Nazir Ahmed, Rashidul Khairi, and *Aab-e-Hayat*, with Mother's permission or under her orders. The magazine *Ismat* would also be read every month line by line under her orders.

Most of the girls at school and college had Madhubala, Nargis, Nimmi, Sabiha Khanum, and Musarrat Nazir as their heroines; while the few literary ones like us thought very highly of the first and newly-published books of Vajida Tabassum and Jilani Bano. We would argue about *Meray bhi Sanam Khanay*, memorize passages from *Kankari* and go to meet Hajira Masrur, who resided near the college, like our heroine.

When we went to Manto Sahib's house wrapped in our burqas for his autograph, I remember he called out loudly: 'Safia, come! There are some girls here.'

In the verandah of Hijab Imtiaz Ali's house, having lifted up my veil, I found myself staring dumbfounded at the Siamese cats, blue curtains and carpets. With Faiz Sahib I had a double, or rather triple-sided, relationship. Chhimi (Salima Hashmi) was one year junior to me in college. We became friends during this time. I knew Mrs Alys Faiz from before because she was the 'Apa Jan' of the *Pakistan Times*. And with Faiz Sahib from 1959 until his death, I had such a passionate relationship that there was no question of the spark of affection ever wavering. During this period under the title 'My Best Short Story' all my favourite short-story writers started broadcasting their stories on the radio. The day *Kala Gulab* was being broadcast and before it started, I found myself flushed, as though the writer was coming to touch me.

1. Portrait, 1955

2. Portrait, 1981

3. With a sculpture made by Leonardo da Vinci, 1993

4. With my sons Mizo and Faisal, 1969

5. The house in Bulandshahr, 1985

6. With Tanveer Masud, Masud, and Yusuf Kamran, 1978

7. With my mother and sisters, 1973

8. In Seville, Spain with Mizo, my elder son, 1999

9. Faisal with his daughter Aisha, 1998

10. At Alhamra, Granada with my daughter-in-law Mariam

11. Marriage turns into mourning, 1984

12. Friends comforting me, 1984

13. Making kebabs with Ashfaque Ahmed, Bano Qudsia, and Aneeq

14. With Dr Aal-e-Ahmed Suroor, Delhi, 1983

15. With Parveen Shakir and a Nepalese poet, Bangladesh, 1991

16. With Farooq Hasan and Munir Niazi, Montreal, 1983

17. With Sehba Lucknawi, Jagannath Azad, and Hasan Abid, Disney land, 1983

18. With Jamiluddin Aali, Himayat Ali Shair, Iftikhar Arif, Parveen Shakir, and Ashfaque Hussain, Norway, 1991

19. With Indian artists, Delhi, 1989

20. With Farida Hafeez, Parveen Shakir, and Ahmed Faraz, Kathmandu, 1990

21. With Dr Gopichand Narang, Delhi, 1987

22. With Syrian and Bangladeshi poets, Bhopal, 1989

23. With German writer Mr Zaipal and Dr Munir, Hamburg, 1993

24. On the Great Wall of China with Rubina Qureshi, 1987

25. With a women's delegation, Bahamas, 1989

26. With the delegates of a women's conference, Nairobi, 1985

27. With Shamim Hanafi and Joshi, Jaipur, 1985

28. With American scholars, Italy, 1992

29. With Faiz Ahmed Faiz, 1974

30. With M.F. Hussain and Ahmed Faraz, 1990

31. With Ali Imam, 1981

32. With Jaun Elia and Majnun Gorakhpuri, 1987

33. With Firdaus Haider, Sibte Hasan, and Salahuddin Haider, 1986

34. With Hijab Imtiaz Ali and Ada Jaffery, 1977

35. With Khalida Hussain and Munir Ahmed Shaikh, 1986

36. With guests at the birthday of the exiled Faiz, 1981

37. With journalist and writer friends in Karachi, 1988

38. With Qateel Shifai and Saqi Farooqi, 1988

39. With Javed Shahin, Ijaz Ahmed, and Kashmiri Lal Zakir, 1985

40. With Dr Ludmila Vasilieva, 1983

41. With Jilani Bano, 1987

42. With Muhammad Umer Memon, 1986

43. With Niaz Ahmed, Zahid Dar, Intizar Hussain, and Shafqat Tanvir Mirza, 1986

44. With women journalists, Khem Karan, 1965

45. With Mumtaz Mufti, Parveen Atif, Dr Saleem Akhter, and Amjad Islam Amjad, 1987

46. With Asghar Nadeem Syed, Munnu Bhai, A.B. Ashraf, Anwar Ahmed, Mehdi Abbas, 1982

47. With Dr Aftab Ahmed, Salimuzzaman Siddiqui, Syed Waqar Azeem, Dr Abdullah Chughtai, Intizar Hussain, Suhail Ahmed Khan, Zahoor ul Akhlaque, and Yusuf Kamran, 1983

48. With Intizar Hussain, Bano Qudsia, and Begum Intizar Hussain, 1981

49. With Taj Saeed, Mustansir, Salahuddin Mahmud, Jamila Hashmi, Intizar Hussain, and Fehmida Riaz, 1980

50. London, 1995

51. Saarc Writers Conference Delhi, 2007

52. With Saky, the South Korean writer, South Korea, 2008

53. At the mausoleum of Benazir Bhutto, 2008

54. With women of Tharparkar, 2007

Marriage certificate, 1960. Unsigned by Kishwar Naheed

Woman of Action

Normally when Kishwar Naheed, 44, the fiery Pakistani poetess travels, a motorcycle and jeep follow her. Ms Naheed is a director in the information department of the government in Lahore. But it is not her job which entitles her to these privileged perks of escorts: she is a vibrant member of the Women's Action Forum (WAF) in Pakistan. For the last few years WAF and other women's organisations have proved to be the only worthy opponents of the mullahs and General Zia-ul Haq—and when the going gets tough for the opposition, they ask the women to be out in front. There are other reasons for which the visit-

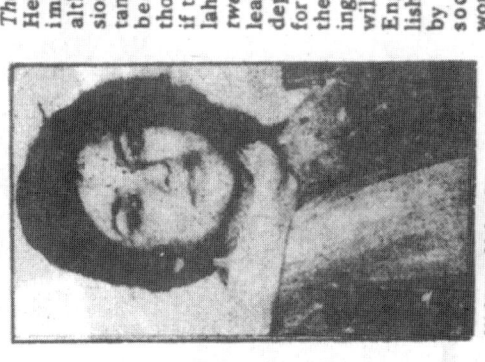

Kishwar Naheed: terror of the mullahs

ing poetess is a special thorn in the flesh of the mullahs and the establishment. She recently translated Simon de Beauvoir's *The Second Sex* into Urdu. Her translated version was immediately banned, although the English version is available in Pakistani book shops. The book became accessible to thousands of women. And if this book upset the mullahs, her new book, *Between Dream and Dust* released on the eve of her departure in mid-March for India, will really send the blood pressure shooting up. This book, which will soon be published in English by Vikas Publishing House (translated by Uma Vasudev), is a sociological study of women in Pakistan. It examines women as unpaid labour in organised sectors of society, in agriculture. Apparently, women comprise only two per cent of the organised sector. Ms Naheed's powerful imag-

ery comes across in her speech, like a whiplash. Example: the boom of health and beauty clubs reminds her of the "slavery of the Moghul period: ten women would massage a woman in the harem to make her soft for the man who had to touch her every evening." On marriage: "What is marriage? If two people agree to make love in front of a hundred people it is legal (whether they want to or not). If on the other hand two people agree to love each other without the hundred people (looking on), it is illegal."

One could go on. Ms Naheed practises what she preaches. Since college she has stopped wearing jewellery, embroidered *kurtas* or make-up except for the occasional dash of lipstick.

حوالہ نمبر ۸۵۲
مورخہ ۲۲ فروری ۱۹۷۳

گواہی

سکریڑی صاحب، پاکستان ریڈ کراس کلڈ خیبر پاکستان

تسلیمات –

یہ خبر انتہائی افسوس ناک ہے کہ پی – ایس – سی
لائیڈ و کے دو مشہور شعراء اور راہنمہ ریڈ کراس کلڈ کے ارکان کو پی – سی
کی دہشت پسند ڈاکٹر شپ سے BLACK کر دیا ہے۔
(پاکستان نا مہ صفحہ ۳ – مورخہ ۲۲ فروری ۱۹۷۳) اور آدمی
ایک ماہ کی بےدخلی تنخواہ دیگر ملازمت سے سبک دوش کر دیا ہے۔
یہ دو شعراء احمد فراز اور کشور ناہید ہیں۔

چونکہ احمد فراز اور کشور ناہید راہنمہ ریڈ کراس کلڈ کے ارکان ہیں۔
اس لیے میں آپ سے درخواست کرتا ہوں کہ ان کی جبری سبک دوشی
پر راہنمہ ریڈ کراس کلڈ اسمبلی ریزولوشن لیشنی پاس کرے۔

میری یہ بھی درخواست ہے کہ کشور ناہید اور احمد فراز
کو مالی مشکلات سے بچا نے کے لیے اپا ہی امداد ور آدمیوں کے بعد

سے کم از کم پہلی بدوں ماہ دو روپیہ وظیفہ مقارر کیے بعد بھی غور فرمایا
جائے – اور اگر ام این تجویز پر مطلب غور کر کا مضمون کچھئی – نیز
اس مسئلہ کی طرف مجلس عاملہ کے دوسری اراکین کو بھی متوجہ کرائی –

خدا آپ کو صحت مند اور جاوید سلامت رکھے –

آپ کا دلی احمد
دستخط منسقی امور سندہ
رکن مجلس عاملہ

منذرہ بالا تجویز جناب الور سندہ کی
ازراہ کرم ازسر برا کر پیش کیجئے از نشست
تیمر سید چشمتی کی تحصیل کیجئے
یہ مسئلہ ربا کا صدر سندہ کے
ارادہ – ٹیکستیلی
6-6
3. 3. 72

Ref. No. 854
22 February 1973

Respected Secretary Sahib
Pakistan Writers Guild, West Pakistan

Dear Sir,

It is very sad news that PNC has sacked two distinguished poets who are members of the Writers' Guild from the resident directorship of PNC (*Pakistan Times*, 22 February 1973, p.3) and that it has relieved them of their responsibilities by giving them one month's advance salary. These two poets are Ahmed Faraz and Kishwar Naheed.

Because Ahmed Faraz and Kishwar Naheed are members of the Writers' Guild, I am requesting you that the Writers' Guild should pass a resolution expressing its sorrow at their forced termination.

I also request that to save Kishwar Naheed and Ahmed Faraz from financial difficulties a monthly stipend of at least Rs 50 from the disabled writers' fund should be considered. I would be grateful if you would consider this proposal.

Please also draw the attention of the other members of the governing body to this suggestion.

May God grant you health and long life.

Yours truly,

Sgnd: Anwar Sadeed
Member governing body

[Handwritten note by Qateel Shifai]

The above proposal is by Mr Anwar Sadeed. Kindly let me have your opinion so that I can carry out Mr Sadeed's orders. In all events this issue will be resolved with your concurrence.

Yours,

Qateel Shifai
3.3.72

Jan 14, 1994

Dear M/s Naheed,

Happy New Year!! I hope you and your sons had a wonderful time together. Daron and I had a tiring and exciting five weeks in the rest of Italy. I have to say Venice was the best. It was like living on a fantasy island. I hope the New Year has brought you only wonderful things thus far. I'm sending the materials you asked for — my lovely creation! You made Bellagio an even more special place to live and inspired me to create something beautiful. Thank you from the bottom of my soul.

Love,
Donna Hagen

P.S. Hope to see you in Pakistan soon.

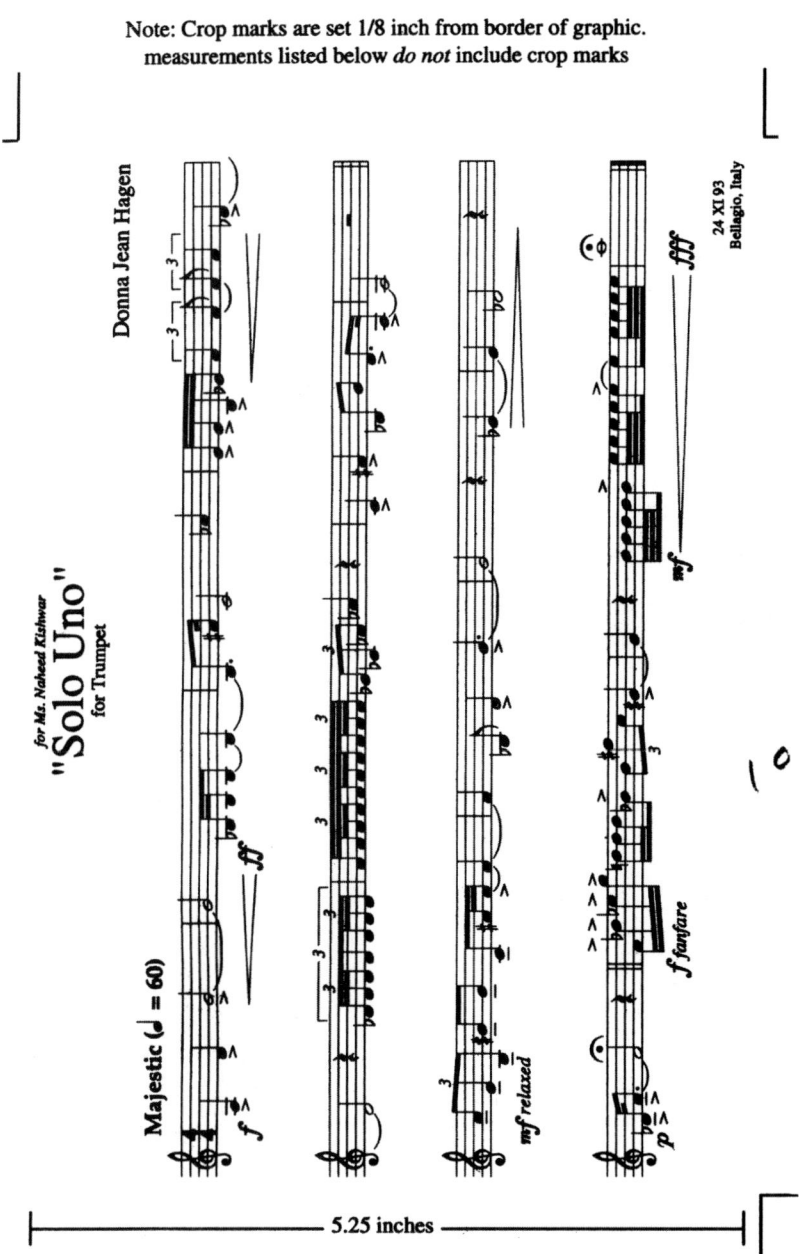

Music composed by American trumpeter, Donna Hagen in Bellagio on Kishwar Naheed's poetry

Caption of cartoon: 'After all, immortality lies in art'; on placard: National Centre; on bag: National Centre. Cartoon by Afshar

Friday, December 14, 1979

By YUNUS AHMAR

Younus Ahmar's article on Kishwar Naheed which was censored along with the accompanying photograph (cutting from *The Muslim*), 1979

Portrait by Bashir Mirza

'Here he is with *Kala Gulab* in his hands!' the announcer said. My heart started racing. The story started. Two minutes later...I turned off the radio and started weeping—the writer's voice was so ugly and his pronunciation so awful that the image I had created of him collapsed with a thud. The stage of crumbling idols had begun.

Chapter Five
First Appearance

Once again we changed homes. We had moved from Garhi Shahu to Santnagar. It looked like some place out in the suburbs. As the house was on the main road it did not give the appearance of a neighbourhood. There was a different atmosphere—many homes large and small in one building—people from UP, Punjabis, Pathans, villagers, city people, school teachers, college boys, office clerks, college girls, all mixed up. What a motley crowd! It was from here that I began to imbibe a mixture of cultural influences. The house was small. We were seven brothers and sisters. There was nothing else to do except read books—in winter wrapped in a quilt in one corner or outside on the rooftop, and in summer hidden in a room.

At college when the mushaira season started a poetess was needed to team up with another. Prior to this it was the custom that *ghazals* of seven couplets would be obtained from some poet or the other, and two girls with beautiful voices would read them out melodically. If they won a trophy or prize the college made a name for itself. End of story. Now, the problem was that there was a poetess in the fourth year and there was me in the first year. I was given the *misra tarah*: 'Sab key hi gareyban see dalay, apna hi gareyban see na sakay' (The robes that were in anguish torn, I sewed them all except my own). I came home with a heavy burden. Having finished my chores and done with studying, I took my quilt to the courtyard and was thinking: *Oh God. How will I complete these verses?* When all of a sudden it seemed that I only had to start the ghazal and it would be done. I started writing and it became morning. Eleven couplets were done. I presented the teacher with the ghazal and by bringing the trophy back to the college, got my name up on the notice board as a poetess.

As I started participating in mushairas, I began to meet writers. Those with whom I had become familiar through the radio, or read about in the newspapers, or whose books I had bought and got autographed, would now present prizes and ask: 'Since when have you been writing?' 'Where do you live?' 'In which year are you studying?'

From now on those who will be mentioned will not just be mentioned by name but as I remember them. Their form, likeness, and image are embodied inside me in their own way. Had this not been the case then after the passage of so much time everything would have got muddled up. After so many summers everything would have got scorched.

'Where do you live?' one judge of a mushaira asked, giving me the prize.

'Near your house.'

'Come over in the evenings, come and meet me.'

Till late at night, even after I had reached home, this phrase kept echoing in my ears: 'Come over in the evenings.' But how? How could I leave the house? I wanted to go, I wanted to meet him—he had invited me himself. 'Mother, he is an elderly gentleman—a retired professor—a poet. Mother, he asked me to come in the evening. Mother, I will study Persian with him. Mother, send my brother along—I'll just go and meet him.'

'I won't go with you. What business do you have with strange men?'

'Listen to me!' Father's voice came from the next room.

I thought Father must also be wanting to meet him. He will take me along. At once I went into his room. He was lying down, writing something. He asked me to sit down on the bed; kept on writing while I kept on simmering. When he had finished, he took off his glasses and said: 'Young lady, you've done enough of mushairas, you've made quite a name for yourself in college, collected quite a few cups. Now do as I say. Whoever it was from whom you took these ghazals, go and return them to him. In your house no one has gone beyond the limits like you have. Have you seen your older sisters? If your mother had to deal with this it would be even worse. So listen to me and stop this drama.'

At every stage of my life, every moment, I have had to hear this phrase: 'In your house nobody has gone over the limits like this. Stop the drama!'

From here on the period of meeting writers on the sly started. In the evening, returning from college or a debate, I would stop over at their places, listen to poetry or show them my own. I would listen to the talk of the people sitting there—old stories, verses written by the masters, commentaries on them—a literary salon. God knows what all would come under discussion—on the one hand, there would be things I wouldn't understand, on the other, I would be clutching my burqa in fear that those at home would level their eyes at me like predators.

Burqa—yes, it was dropped over my head at the age of seven and stayed until my university days. At college and university, abandoning the burqa in the ladies room, I would take part in debates and mushairas, then put it on again before going home. Once a huge picture of me receiving a prize was published in some newspaper. I was really in the soup. I had to use up all my pocket money: my younger brothers and sisters, the neighbourhood kids, relatives, were making a beeline for the house with the newspaper! I had to beg them: 'Don't let Mother and Father know. Burn the paper ... hide it ... save me!'

In those days (1960) only a few newspapers were published. Photographs and reports of debates were given prominence. I too received an offer from one newspaper to send in reports from colleges. *We'll give you a cycle and 75 rupees a month.* I was ecstatic. But all hell broke loose at home. I was still wearing the burqa, how could I possibly ride a cycle? And then a friend of mine who rode a bike had divorced her husband during her college days. She was a bad woman. How could a Syed girl behave like this?

I didn't get permission to work for the newspaper but I did get permission to take part in the university programme on the radio. It was here that my friendship began with the creators of the new style of poetry and new poetic expressions. Now new authors and new books became my fellow travellers.

The atmosphere on radio at that time was a very cultured one, steeped in learning and literature. All the producers were poets or writers and appreciated the fundamentals of music. My acquaintance with all the eminent male and female singers of today, musicians, and maestros began at that time. It is such an amazing friendship that even today we are like family. In those days all the programmes were broadcast live. I often heard singers singing their latest ghazals in front of me in the studio. What was amusing was that in order to achieve fame at the hands of these artistes, the smart producers who were not poets would use work borrowed from others to make their name. And do so till today.

If you look at the levels of friendship, what exists between college girls is simple friendship: the camaraderie of studying together; of preparing notes together. They were not bothered about literature. At university too the people who took part in debates together or read mushairas would become friends. Then there were the friends who would sit in one corner in a restaurant making out, while we sat in another corner. Of the two parties, the members who arrived first would often share the moments of waiting together. They would accept messages for each other too. Then the circle of friendships widened and every acquaintance started claiming to be a friend. Every pipsqueak who you may have met once with affection would bandy your friendship about. And friends are so sweet—if someone is criticizing you they listen quietly to everything and just smile, they never say anything themselves!

Having taken part in debates I had already been acclaimed as an orator. In debates we made use of memorized speeches written in the old classical language. On the one hand, there was the zest for the language and on the other, the moment I entered a mixed debate, I would announce that the girls hadn't come to receive the consolation prize. We would participate in the general debate. If we got the prize in the general debate then well and good, but favours were not acceptable. This was not a ruse. From the beginning, I despised the word favour and its association with being inferior. If you were not capable then why complain, or talk of rights?

This same thought has been with me my whole life. Why complain? What rights? But what if you did not get your rights even when you were entitled? I have seen this so often and in so many situations. My friend got married and went to England. Her husband, who had been touted as a bar-at-law, was living on unemployment allowance. She worked hard to bring home the butter and chickens. But behind her back, he would rub the butter on his body and boil the chickens and eat them. After having come to England in his youth, he had tested his manhood on all kinds of women. But in the process he had lost his vigour and become impotent. Now by rubbing butter on his body and eating chickens he was hoping to restore his potency as all the doctors had given up hope. This good woman would return home after having put in overtime and he would beat her up demanding to know who she had been with. When she asked this impotent, good-for-nothing for divorce he would beat her black and blue. If she talked about going back to her country he would hide her passport.

I also saw girls, who were much older than me and very beautiful, refusing to go back to their husband's or in-laws' house after one night. When I grew up I found out that all those 'liberated' men, once they had tired of having a good time and become useless and wanted to settle down, would be offered these maids who had been sitting at home waiting for their knights in shining armour. The girls who were too outspoken would come back home and the rest would cover their heads, put a seal on their lips, and eke out their life.

Although we had been stopped even from meeting our male cousins, the girls at college would tell the strangest stories about their relationships and affairs. They would read out their letters while I would be left feeling miserable. But this misery and this feeling of being left out did not continue for long because I had started writing poetry and was now receiving letters from editors. If their matter-of-fact letters were embellished with some verses or illustrations, this in itself would seem very romantic. If they strayed even a little bit into the realm of informality—'A woman who writes so well, how nice must she be herself?'—sentences such as these would make you crumble. While standing on the parapet if some crazy guy happened to glance at you it would make your day. In those days we didn't know why during such moments men would bring the end of their *dhotis* up between their legs and wear it tucked up like drawers. Why *paan* eaters would make the sounds they did while spitting out betel juice; why smokers would inhale so deeply, why men would keep undoing the buttons of their shirt and rub their hands on their chests.

At college burning incense during the inter-collegiate debates would create a wonderful atmosphere. Those of us who were experienced orators would vie to be the last to speak, so that we could benefit from the points of the previous speakers in preparing our text; we felt this was important. When we had entered this field as novices we had tried to have ourselves positioned at the beginning so that we could mention all the new points and get over with our speech before the judges had got tired. It was these mixed debates and mushairas that got rid of any remaining shyness in me or fear of men. We would all go from college as a team, chat, pass witty remarks and tell jokes. We had a free hand with the Annual Day, Literary Week and magazine: the teachers would neither come and ask us what we were doing nor would we give them a report or ask if we could publish such and such a ghazal or not.

But all this strutting about was limited to the boundary walls of the college and university. The moment I came home I had to hide the cups I had won in the debates and mushairas inside the flour canister or in the garbage bin, to save my skin. Or else on seeing the cup there would be such a ruckus: 'Here she comes having brought disgrace on the family name! Had I known you would turn out like this I would have strangled you at birth!'

Let me ask you, Mother. Have you ever seen your daughters suffocating? When their own children are turned into snakes in the grass and set against them, and the father, having completed his quota of torture, heaves a sigh of relief. When manhood is only felt to be vindicated by hanging women on the gallows of blame. When your daughters ask for their rights only to get slaps and kicks, and oilcans with matches are their fate. When they are made to adorn beds against their will, and called chaste. When cigarettes are stubbed out on their bodies and a price is put on the moans of a burning body. When they accept a man's impotency out of shame or as society's norms and keep on smiling. But no one is willing to give any importance to *their* needs. When brothers also look on their sisters with lust and if the sister reveals it then she herself is held to be guilty, the brother free again, unbridled and innocent. When fathers themselves are aroused by a daughter's affection and his lust begins to grow inside her body, then even in front of the doctor she is unable to point her finger at the culprit. When every stain of immodesty is a blot only on the forehead of a woman and every rape is proof of manliness—a man is after all like a stallion; having washed, changed, neat and clean, he makes his rounds from house to house. While the woman is left with the consolation:

an elephant may roam from place to place but will always come back to its home.

This is also held to be a woman's fate that religion, culture, and humanity are used on behalf of men and against women. Sometimes her exploitation is in the name of beauty; sometimes in the name of intelligence, or wealth, or even poverty. Even when God is identified, it is as male. Jesus went on the cross; his breath was said to heal and give life. But Mary who gave *him* life is only garlanded in pictures. When the Prophet (PBUH) came to Madinah, Hazrat Umar (RA) complained about the shrewdness of the women there and said that they were teaching his wife to answer back. No one mentions these examples or talks about these women. In order to give credibility to the mischievous and false story of the grain of wheat, woman was called a temptress or a seducer at will. Sometimes heaven would be deemed to be beneath her feet and sometimes her intelligence would be ridiculed as being in her corns! Sometimes marriage against her will was held to be unlawful. But more often, with her head forcibly bowed, under the din of congratulations and blessings, she would be tied to the coattails of a wolf she hadn't seen before. That would be considered lawful. Jokes, anecdotes, humour would all be linked to women and make the teller feel macho.

This desire to feel macho is a stone which greets a woman at every step with a sharp jab. During college days, despite giving me the first prize in the inter-collegiate debates, the venerable guest poet would invariably say: 'Come and meet me. We will talk. Show me your poetry.'

When I would ask: 'Why, is there something wrong with it?' Then taken aback, he would reply: 'No, there's nothing wrong with it. But there's no harm in showing it and getting advice from the masters.'

All the masters would be vying to claim you as their protégé; or else they would stamp all over you. How is she daring not to be a devotee, when we have spent our whole life collecting disciples on our respective mounds? Each master would ooze humility. When asked 'Have *you* given her these verses? They are brilliant. They reek of your skill,' the respected master laughs indulgently and answers: 'One has to do it.'

In the same way as when a woman humiliates a man and pushes him out of her house or room, to hide his disgrace, he says: '*Arre yaar*, she wouldn't even let me get up. It's with great difficulty that I've come out.'

The desire for a slave kept appearing before me in many different guises: in friendship, at the office, poetry, marriage... to the extent that the moment my sons grew up and became taller than me I had to be their slave. Then chastity, modesty, manners, decency are all in tact. But if you don't accept it then the sins of the whole world are waiting like an open-mouthed crocodile to gobble you up. *If you are a journalist then sit with me and have some tea. Or at least talk affectionately.* If he is a scoundrel and turns it into a scandal, just swallow it. Then you'll be a good girl. Otherwise you are a fifth columnist, unpatriotic, and whatever else they want you to be.

A western woman also goes out looking to become someone. But what happens is that the man becomes an officer, the woman is the secretary. The man is the manager, the woman the telephone operator, the man is the doctor the woman is the nurse, the man is the pilot, the woman is the airhostess, the man is king, the woman enters into the harem and starts walking on the path of religion. Women writers are discussed in line with their rank (i.e. their husband's rank). If the husband is a high-ranking official then the woman writer is everyone's 'sister-in-law', sweet, pious, and with all the right domestic skills. If the husband is not such a high-ranking official then from her writing to her character everything is suspect. She also gets marks for beauty. The response and logic being that at least looking at her does you good. In social gatherings or in private they may praise a woman to high heavens but when faced with her at work they do a complete about turn and talk down at her. When you ask the reason for this contradiction at once you are reassured: 'People will talk. Then how will we meet? I can't live without you, that's why I had to steel myself to say all these things. Please forgive me, my love, please forgive me.'

There are very few people who have a sense of shame. The chair bestows such an aura that the most oafish officer seems to be a paragon of poetry, love, beauty, intelligence, and wit and the coquettes gather around as though he was an intimate friend, to cheapen their beauty. I have seen such beauties throwing themselves at the most leprous officers and ministers that it is hard to give credence to what the eyes have seen. A few thousand rupees is all the night requires. They met at dinner. He said 'I'll drop you home.' *'Aahen bhi bhari shikwe bhi kiye...'* ('I sighed, I complained...'). It's a strange breed that organizes musical gatherings and tributes of beauty for those in power. And these latter, like uncrowned kings, move forward head held high, and all doors keep opening one by one.

The small fry are the ones who run brothels, who ask for ten to a hundred rupees for showing a girl's face. And when the girl is chosen, off she goes to fulfil the demands of pleasure. Morning sees the broken bodies tossing and turning on sagging beds. I went especially to see this area in Bombay: a room as small as one string bed, soiled curtains all around it, and in the middle of the bed the pleasure-giver, who dies of a sexual disease or coughing up blood. In all the cities of Europe the image of these districts is quite different. There, in a glass showcase, a woman dressed in a skimpy top stands invitingly. She has a similar small room but shiny and a showcase. Here too imperialism shows its true colours: most of the women are black. Those who go looking at them are also often wheat-complexioned. In the Philippines and Thailand a big source of national income are those girls who sell the most drinks or nights. Before night has even fallen these bars open, a flock of girls wait at the doors to trap the passerby and get their commission. They don't get any salaries. This commission is their daily allowance. Like the '*chotas*' of the cafes and hotels of my country who run from morning till evening, just for your tip, bringing tea, *naan*, *cholay*, fish, Coca Cola, and paan. But this is still better than the unfortunates wrapped around the pillars in America and London who wait on the streets and quote a different figure for every hour, and get used up.

Whether it is Bombay or some other city there are also those who come out at night to supply the neighbourhoods with women and in the morning are back in their homes. The people who light these lamps of desire are very respectable in the eyes of the world. Gogol calls them flies, not humans.

Chapter Six
First Slip

After moving to Pakistan I would see after every eight days the floors being washed, embroidered sheets and pillow cases being laid out, kebabs and halwas prepared and women of all types coming in. It turned out that today this sister had received a proposal, tomorrow that one. Oh God, why did these people turn up day in and day out? Why didn't these proposals come to anything? Eventually I found out that they were looking for respectable boys, sons of Syeds. A Syed girl could not be given to a different caste. Then I remembered all those aunts who had grown old sitting at home, spending their days and nights working on their sheets and their bodies with their own hands.

Seeing my older sisters go through this I vowed to myself: I am not going to marry the kind of respectable boys or Syed boys, the completely stupid ones, that my family bring home. But then what should I do? This thought would frighten me...

Knock! Knock! 'Who is it?'

'Go and see,' Mother said. A little later my brother came back and said angrily: 'It's the editor of a paper. He's come to meet you.'

'But I haven't called anyone. I didn't give anyone my address. I haven't met anyone,' I tried to exonerate myself before the whole household. Every eye was on me. Everywhere there was hatred. Against me.

My brother shouted again. 'Yesterday you read a poem at some mushaira. He's come to ask for the poem. You told him that we live in Santnagar. You took the first prize from his hand.'

The next day he went to the head of the college. The principal sent for me. He introduced me proudly and said: 'Give him your prize-winning poem.'

Then surreptitiously I went in my burqa to the office of the monthly and climbed up the stairs. New vistas were opening up for me. However, seeing another burqa-clad woman sitting there I returned on my heels. God knows why in those days the houses and offices of most writers and artistes were only accessible by stairs. Ihsan Danish, Bokhari Sahib, Faiz Sahib, Soofi Sahib, Hafeez Sahib, Josh Sahib, Chughtai Sahib, and later on as well there were many artists who you could only meet by climbing stairs.

Eeny, meeny, miny moe/Catch a tiger by its toe... I got enrolled in my masters. In the whole university and Government College there were only two of us poetesses. We thought no end of ourselves. We started getting letters every day at the university address. This was the first time I was getting letters addressed to me. I was scared. I showed them to the girls who were with me, then the boys also saw them. At 11 o'clock in the lawn in front of the department, we would all read together the letters which had been written by boys from different departments in the university. Then the boys from my department would go and tease them. Among all these boys there was one who was very handsome. Different too.... I would come out of my house to go to college, and he would be standing ten paces ahead of me—with his cycle—waiting. I would go to the library; when I came out he would be waiting. I would go to a mushaira. He would come and stand right in front of me. He would smile—one familiar face among the dozens of unfamiliar ones. All my fear would vanish. I would feel safe. The British Council Library was some distance away. I would walk to it; he would accompany me. On the way back he would say: 'Let's have tea.'

The Coffee House had some stairs that went up. Many couples would be sitting there. He and I would go there too. Sometimes the revolutionaries sitting downstairs would come up when they spotted him and chat with us. It was one more place to meet liberals, communists, labour leaders, student leaders, and writers.

Playing hide and seek—making the excuse of going to the library, of studying, a different kind of study. *Eeny, meeny, miny moe/Catch a tiger by its toe*—making a programme—a girl friend, he, and I made a trip to Murree. In Murree too it was the same routine: mushairas, discussions, get-togethers, meetings with writers. Our romance was still at this stage when my brother told on me. Coffee House, British Council, Murree, the cat was out of the bag. A hasty engagement and wedding was arranged.

The bride who was married with half a seer of *laddoos* was accompanied by one sack of books and another of the cups she had won as prizes. She had one set of clothes on her body.

We got into a tonga and arrived at a house in Abbott Road. It had the same ambience of the house in Santnagar but was slightly more like a film set. Each room was occupied by a different tenant. Our wedding night was also strange. We both felt like thieves; both were a little scared. Neither he nor

I was prepared for this marriage which had taken place after we had been given half an hour to make our decision. Neither his family nor his friends knew about it. My punishment for not marrying a Syed boy was being meted out to him as well.

This is not true. Men don't get punished for anything. It's only the woman who gets punished. He knew that I didn't want to marry a Syed boy; that I don't want to live in this oppressive environment; that I run away from rituals; that I talk about revolution; that I want to work.

He fulfilled all my wishes. We started living in the same house, two free spirits. I, free to take up responsibilities; he on a motorbike instead of a cycle, then in a car.... *Eeny, meeny, miny moe/Catch a tiger by its toe....* He was so handsome—in his car—waiting for someone else. Within one year the places he would wait at and the people he would be waiting for would have changed.

Someone who has learnt from the moment she came into this world to save the garnished *daal* for the brothers and father, and give everyone else the dregs from the bottom of the pan, who has seen the gravy with meat doled out to the men and the gravy with potatoes to the rest of the house, finds both the modern and the traditional woman growing inside her, tearing each other to bits. She advocates the right of women to be equal but at the same time won't see any man in the house washing the dishes, sewing a button, ironing, polishing his shoes. Rather she won't allow him to do so. She will kill herself but go on doing all the work. Unlike the housewives, she doesn't greet her husband on his return with a handkerchief tied around her head bemoaning her fate. If there is a wedding in the family she doesn't give her husband an ultimatum: bring home such and such amount of cash then I'll be able to attend your sister's wedding, or else you go alone. And the poor husband out of shame scurries about arranging for the money, feeling terrified of his wife. The wife who is herself employed is aware of the household income. If arrangements have to be made she'll do it herself. It is solely to feed the egos of their husbands that the housewives are acting out this drama that they don't know where the road leads, or where it comes from. They can't go to the bank, they can't go to the bazaar, they don't know how to carry on a conversation. The men themselves exaggerate the hypocritical oppression of women.

It is in a man's nature that by spending money on a woman he gets a sense of his responsibilities. He feels her in his possession. But the truth of the matter—whether he loves her or not—is never revealed.

But when is the truth ever revealed? At work the officers are told: Go and stay in the rural areas for ten days to find out the problems of the villagers. But who does it? One night at the rest house and back in the morning. They claim their expenses for two days' and one night's stay and are back home. If it's a teacher then she takes half the salary, gives half to the clerk and relaxes at home. Who is going to get any work out of the *patwaris* and *naib tehsildar*? In the efforts to save their lands everyone will be relying on the advice of these people in order to define the boundaries. Working on a salary of Rs 5000 and an allowance of Rs 50,000, the officer will be regarded as a government servant. If the army needs to be praised so be it. The army only gets paid for standing by in case there is a war.

If you want praise for your adherence to Islam it's easy: 'I have to send my wife for Haj.' If the wife has to be taken for sightseeing then the (official) tour must include all those places where the wife wants to go. If there is a wedding in the family you'll be ordered to work on a holiday. And the boss, having eaten the wedding food, will ring you up: 'Close up the office now. Go home. I have got fed up of meeting people on your behalf. Do your job with care, it took me a long time to restore your reputation in the city. These women have been very clever in agitating for their independence. They want to free themselves of restrictions, to come and go as they please. No one should question them. They should be free to drink, smoke, have sex, mix with men.'

If someone screams at them: 'Shut up!' Then they backtrack: 'You took it the wrong way. *Arre* what are you doing? Come. I am on my own. Come and have tea. We'll sit together.'

There is one phrase I hear practically every day—as an insinuation, allusion, openly or as a favour, in different guises. Sometimes it is 'You don't look your age. You look like a college student even today'; or 'This colour really suits you'; or 'Today you are looking very fresh'; or 'You look ravishing even in this simplicity.' The woman will blush and smile, no matter at what stage of her life she is.

This trait of blushing is quite remarkable in men as well. We got all the pending work at the office through our bosses with the greatest of ease by complimenting them on their looks, their ties, and listening to the stories of the wild oats they sowed in their youth. We would keep encouraging them with morsels. Wow! You must have been quite an athlete! That's all it took for them to begin salivating and regale us with stories of their daredevil youth while we got our files from the stenotypist and placed them in front one by one. Little white lies but doing so much good. The cases of the poor employees would be cleared. Everyone would bless us and the bosses themselves would be happy and spout charming sentences dripping with poetry.

While editing a magazine you get to see a rag-bag of people. Writers who come from the rural areas bring sugarcane juice, coriander oil, molasses halwa, tins of ghee or handloom cloth, according to what they can afford, and the poor editor keeps these things to humour them. If the editor is a woman then all of a sudden it dawns on people that she is a very intelligent woman. To win her over, all the writers make the time to visit. The young writers send their work to her and have the replies framed up, as the foundation of a strong relationship. Then there are those champions who display recently received letters under the glass top of their table so that everyone can see that they receive letters too.

The moment your official responsibilities end many friendships come to an end as well. Your intelligence also becomes suspect. And evenings spent with you also decrease. People now flock to the door of the new editor and are seen presenting them with their work. On the pretext of publishing the work of a certain poet, my friends and I had fish fingers at his expense on many occasions. And he didn't get upset because his work was being published with great gusto.

Like editors of magazines, radio and television producers also know how to get people to make much of them. The moment the programme is aired, the compere and the performer will fork out gifts ranging from dinner invitations to cloth pieces for trousers and suits as the dues of friendship. And sometimes the producer, like the naib tehsildar, will make his preferred mode of compensation clear. After all, an introduction merits a return. There is one reason why our country appears to provide the most comfortable life, and that is bribery. Every legal and illegal work can be accomplished in our country through bribery. Whether you want a certificate confirming that you are a Muslim or whether it's a character reference from the police station. In this there is no distinction between a *mullah* or a constable. Just hand over the money and get the desired document at home.

This chain of demands is so long that when I started teaching the children they would complain: 'We won't get any marks from your teaching. We'll only get marks from the tuition given by the teacher.'

But why? The answer: 'That's what the teacher says.'

If you try to convince them you get the comment: 'You are turning us into moral cowards.'

And there was some truth in this. When I arranged the tuition, the same child who was shown as passing every subject with grace marks was passing with a position. This situation doesn't end in primary or high school but appears in college and university at a higher price. There is a price for examination centre manuscripts and changing the exam papers in the possession of the teachers. There is bargaining at the stage of preparation of the marks and a price for obtaining the degree without studying; and despite having taken a lecturer's salary all ones life, being notorious for never attending a class, and getting promotion upon promotion, by sucking up to people.

Sucking up was common at work: making it an article of faith to wear whatever pleased your boss whether it was a waistcoat, *sherwani*, *kurta*, shalwar, or suit; or striking up a friendship with the wife of the head of the department; then bringing her VCRs, films, pickles and chutneys, jams and gifts; going shopping together and, if possible, digging out some distant relationship. The whole rigmarole begins afresh when the officer changes. New amusements are chosen depending on their temperament and if turning up every evening with your wife at the boss's house is necessary to keep the job, then doing so with diligence.

If the wife is employed then she'll have to keep on good terms both with her own boss as well as her husband's. From feasts to flattery all have to be dished out with a liberal hand. Many tricks are used to test a woman's employment and to render it suspect. The first is to play the card of familiarity and to convince her of how useful you can be in her private life. Then the most amazing assertion: 'Meeting you I realized for the first time what it means to have a spiritual companion!' Or 'Is your husband also aware then of your boundless talents?' And if they detect any feeling of inferiority in the husband then out comes the trump card: 'Your poor husband is only known because of you!'

On his side the husband, in spite of knowing that the wife doesn't give a fig for these stupid remarks, takes them as an affront to his manhood and immediately sets about asserting his authority. He starts feeling that whatever she does, whether in the home or outside, for the children or for him, is to show him up. Sometimes this suspicion may erupt just on seeing her talk: 'How you talk—what do you take yourself for? You are not the boss everywhere. We are not your servants.'

Or else when the telephone rings and someone asks: 'Is the Begum Sahiba at home?' Pat comes the answer: 'This is a home, not her office. Talk to her at the office.' Then, turning around: 'So now the phones have started coming for you at home too.'

So, was it from a lover then, or was it simply to do with the office work?

'No, this won't happen! Your phones—you can do whatever you want at the office, not at home. Enough!'

I wonder who invented the word liaison. During college days the editor of a journal came to the house to pick up a ghazal. Everybody took it to be a liaison. On the radio, during the students programme, the producer got me to read a ghazal. He came to leave me to the house, tried to establish a liaison. I talked to my boss. The boss and everyone else took it to be a liaison. At some dinner I chatted with someone in a familiar way. That was enough to strengthen the liaison. I talked sincerely to someone on the phone. The next day there he is: 'Yesterday after talking on the phone I wanted to meet you.'

And there is no distinction here—from telephone technicians to distinguished and learned gentlemen, there is a style of giving blessings which requires the hand to reach out for a woman's waist. Saintliness drips from his *surma*-lined eyes.

But if you look at him the writing is clear: an invitation, a blatant invitation to ascend different heights.

What did life give me for taking up an invitation—a dower of Rs 500, a sleepless wedding night, sitting alone on the steps of the house watching life go by and inside, the snores of the man of the house; breakfast in the morning on credit and roaming the streets the whole day; moving from house to house in search of a job; midday—lunch on credit; in the evening threats by the in-laws: 'You'll get picked up—leave our boy.' Then waking up at 5 in the morning to do the housework, then university, then office, then the bus, then housework, then being a wife—like a runaway train.

The days scattered and flew like carded wool, leaving me like an old compressed mattress. When did it start? Since the time the Syed boys stopped proposing for Syed girls, and had to be found by putting advertisements in the papers. The family had scattered. After moving from one country to another, there was no kith and kin, no acquaintance, no reputation or honour to be preserved. In any case, from the time the country was made, honour began to be considered as another term for cowardice. Women threw off their burqas saying: 'Who is there to see?' Honest people started taking bribes saying: 'Who will wag their finger at us?' Those who had nothing broke open and occupied fully furnished homes—there was no one around who had known them for generations. They became Syeds, they became rich, they had families, but they didn't become human beings. Searching for a human being needed an advertisement in the papers but this didn't stop all the louts, and those who were looking to be 'kept' sons-in-law, from turning up with the excuse 'The entire family got left behind. All we have are you people and your family.' One or two meetings and they were confident that they would be a part of the household eating eggs and parathas. One or two claimed to be poets. But poets had got discredited in our house. What had happened was that when the uncles and brothers returned from Aligarh their friends, especially the poet types, would also come home with them. One of them, who could sing very well too, ran off with a cousin. This was some time after the Second World War. I only came to find out about this scandal when I grew up and my own sins were being recounted. From that time on poets were held to be good-for-nothing.

A few days after the marriage the single room in which we stayed was taken away from us thanks to the in-laws. Now we were on the streets. Sometimes we would have to spend the night in the cramped room of a servant and the day in the office or on the street; sometimes we would spend the night at a servant's friend's shop and leave it at dawn; sometimes we would spend the night at a friend's on the excuse that it had got so late, how could we go home in the cold. At last we got a rented house and were in a position to pay the rent. The routine was still the same. In the morning housework, then university, then the office, then home. Every hour of the night would be marked by bitter words: 'So-and-so looked at you today', 'So-and-so put his hand on your shoulder', 'So-and-so put the food on your plate', 'So-and-so came', 'So-and-so didn't come.' In this line-up there were some who were older, some who were the same age, and some younger. The whole night would be spent floundering in the sea of recrimination, then in the morning once again the housework, then university...until I felt the first bud of spring blossoming inside me. The continuous work and stress strangled it. The five-month old foetus had to be taken out in the hospital through an operation, another source of grief.

Now the hospital became a part of my vocabulary. The beds lying on the corridors brought by the patients themselves and the patients who, having had abortions, would bring bun and tea from the canteen in front and have the hospital curry for lunch and dinner, and be grateful; I too was one of them. The husband had deposited them in the hospital like people deposit money in the bank. With no one of their own. No hope. After being released from the hospital I came home as I would from my office. This became such a habit that when I gave birth to my children too the first holiday I took was the day the child was born and when I had an abortion I went from the office and returned to the same chair in the office. On the other hand, I saw women, who having stayed one night, would not get out of bed. The husband is fussing over them; bringing them milk; massaging them; smiling shyly and offering his apologies. The woman is even more doleful. As soon as he leaves she sits up. When you question her about it, she says you have to do it to keep the husband under your thumb. In the same way as the woman who spends the whole day gossiping in the bazaar, at a neighbour's, or in the hospital, then the moment it's evening and she sees the husband approaching ties the dupatta around her head, picks up the broom and is a picture of hard work. The husband snatches the broom away, puts her back on the bed and immediately starts drawing up the patient chart. Both are hypocrites—the husband is coming back after having been with his friends, or at a film show, or dinner, or after having dropped a girl home from the show. He is trying to cover up his peccadilloes and the wife hers. But God keeps everyone's secrets.

However, whoever wants to work and can do so is told: 'Do you call this work?' You work at an office. 'Do you call this work?' You read and write. 'Do you call this work? These penniless writers just have to see a woman's face and they will be full of praise.' If you work on the radio then the comment: 'Now people are asking: "Has your wife become a singing girl?" What can I say? I'll have to stop mixing with respectable people.' If you appear on television then the taunt: 'What's the difference between you and a model? She displays herself in her own way and you in yours.' However, if he goes himself then no doubt it's because he's so talented.

Going to chair meetings in small towns also led to several new paths opening. In these towns, through loudspeakers and in mosques, announcements were made that men's meetings could not be chaired by a woman. Posters were put up. University teachers appealed to government servants to mobilize themselves. Despite all these prohibitions and hurdles there were functions; I got a chance to meet students—girls and boys—to have discussions, to get a feel for their problems, to listen to them. These opportunities were memorable, and will continue to be so, because the girls of these areas, women and sisters, by coming to my functions got the opportunity of being included in a meeting. It is the first stone and the first step that is always difficult. After that keeping the example in front you can move forward.

That too was the first step when we had gone to develop the villages, tiny villages with one-roomed houses where man and buffalo stayed together; kids running naked on the streets, the women cutting fodder after having returned from the fields. No bathing or washing, or changing your clothes, or combing your hair: in the vocabulary of the village all these words were termed 'fashion'. When we would ask our sisters to wash their children's hands and faces they would laugh or scold us or make some rude remarks and turn away. When we would catch hold of the kids and wash their faces, comb their hair, teach them to read, the parents would call us 'mad' and laugh saying: 'You're going to get fed up in a few days.' The interesting thing was that there was so much dislike of city people, and especially of women without burqa, that the village women would ritually cleanse the bed on which we had been sitting as though we had been Christians. The amazing thing was that none of the women in the village wore burqas. However, if the man of the house became a *numberdar*, *choudhry* or chairman of the union council, to distinguish that house from the others, a hessian curtain would go up and the women of the house would start wearing black burqas. With the change in status they would also stop meeting the common women.

Even now it is very difficult to teach the girls in the villages to read and write. The common view is that the moment a girl learns to write she will start writing to boys. As it is, while the family radio can be taken to the fields, or placed in the community centre, a girl cannot listen to it in the house. A girl can wander about the whole village but she can't go out to study. The girl who becomes a teacher and returns to the village finds herself having to submit to all kinds of tests. If the girl has acceptable looks then from the numberdar to the choudhry, they will all want her to have relations with them and be on friendly terms. If her looks are so-so then her working in the village is tantamount to spreading evil. If a girl is good looking and pious and doesn't fall in the numberdar's clutches she is denounced as incapable and loose. Those who cave in are then restricted to their house. They go on receiving a salary in the name of the school. The day someone comes to inspect the school, the children of the house and neighbourhood are collected for a show of hands. The easy way out is to accept the clerk's conditions and not go to the village at all, just divide up the salary, half and half.

There are many images in my mind of the conditions in the village: the one where the girls would veil themselves before us unveiled women; then the one where all the girls would want to consult their 'Baji' before agreeing to any proposal; when the men of the area also would tell us 'Baji, please listen to my 'woman' before you go', and what the 'woman' wanted to know was how to produce less children. I also remember when the fire of hatred between the village and city women was reduced to ashes the day I cooked *makai ki roti*. The women thought my cooking rotis was a miracle. They thought a city woman is just a doll for display. They don't know that the city woman's intellect keeps her going with a smile on her face despite the cruelty and callousness of time. It is the same intellect that forces her to become a doll or a puppet, or at times keeps her from rebelling, despite knowing everything. Not so that when she dies people will say how forbearing she was, she bore it all with a smile. But because she knows that wherever you go and however you go you have to keep asking the questions for which there are no answers.

Chapter Seven
Mahlaqa's Tale

You must have heard about the Mexican girl Laloka who died at the age of three. When her last rites were taking place in the church she leapt up and clung to the rafters shrieking: 'Don't touch me!' Seeing this her own family refused to take her back and for a long time she stayed among animals.

From the age of three I too have been Laloka. All my clearest and sharpest memories date back to this period. I remember I was three when I rolled down from the stairs leading to the roof and fell into the metal dish used for kneading flour. I didn't get hurt, nor did anyone see me; shaken, I went and lay down on my bed. Whenever I wanted to cry on my own, or didn't want to talk to anyone, or wanted to grumble, I would lie down on my bed and pretend to be asleep but this manner of gaining privacy came to an end when my husband's family accepted me as their daughter-in-law. They all came and started living with me—the father-in-law, mother-in-law, sisters-in-law, the mother-in-law's sister's family. You could cook tons of food, it would be gone in a twinkling. If I said anything, at once they'd be on the warpath. 'What do we care about reading and writing? Do we have no self-respect that we should eat off a woman's earnings? Oh, our poor boy has gone mad. He has no shame. He doesn't say anything to her. One day she is learning to drive, the next day she is going off to the radio station. Sometimes she's writing poetry and sometimes she's guffawing with the men.'

Yes, if I quarrelled about their boy gallivanting with American and local women and coming home at two in the morning, my mother-in-law would say: 'Going out is what men do. Our boys are so good looking the girls throw themselves at them. Are they eunuchs or what? What's the harm if they meet them? An elephant may roam from place to place but will always come back to its home.'

The elephant would turn into a tiger on hearing this. Then revert to his old habits. Slaps and punches would become the daily routine of this Prince Charming. When orators run out of logic they turn to poetry; when criminals can't think of anything else they resort to abuses and punches. And if you retaliate then it's on everyone's lips; like Yazid, the oppressor goes around crying about injustice.

What kind of hell is this that the woman who works in ten houses every day should also have to warm the bed at night and should give over her day's earnings for the bottle that fuels the man's lust? I was shaken when my maid servant returned to work the day after giving birth. Her story was that giving birth was no big deal. There was no one to say to her in a melodramatic voice 'You've made me a father, oh, how lucky I am!' Her luck was made up of all the bruises and fasts which were her life in spite of working all day.

The house is a unit of the neighbourhood. Each person has his eye on the other, less to help and more to find fault. If the seller of old bottles goes from the threshold into the courtyard, the neighbours know how long it took him to come out. If a neighbour laughs and chats with the vegetable seller and if the same man dispenses with another woman in a hurry, then this also is known to the neighbours. Who comes to whose house, who goes where, who eats what and meets whom. The neighbours know more about this than the woman of the house herself. If she is a working woman then the women of the whole neighbourhood will be aware of what time she sets off for her office or for school. They will all leave their work and come to the wall, rooftop, blinds, or windows to watch her. Meeting you months later, on some occasion, they will say: 'I still remember such and such sari or outfit of yours.' The poor office worker or school teacher, on the other hand, leaves in such a hurry that she doesn't even remember in the evening what she had worn that morning.

The mind teaches you the art of forgetting many things, otherwise you would go mad with the voices echoing inside. Perhaps that's why when a woman leaves her cramped quarters and returns all dolled up in the evening her husband doesn't say anything. He also likes the children's new clothes and the new stuff in the house and the neighbour has to make several trips to remind him of his promise to accompany her to the market.

Trips also have to be made by the neighbour who time and again sees a stranger entering the next-door house. Then she takes his address and having said to him, 'Don't tell my friend. Today "he"[1] has gone on a tour,' invites the stranger to break down the moss-ridden walls of her life. The grand houses have it good. There, apart from women who've been through six or ten husbands and are in the habit of double-crossing friends, there's a great demand for those who are having a ball after leaving one or two husbands.

In the villages also the husband whose wife has run off with her lover goes to the police station in disgrace and appeals: 'Please sir, my children will run wild. Their mother has run off with so and so. Bring her back!' Or, if he has the strength, he may get the money together to give her a divorce and then more money to make jewellery for another wife and bring her home. Love and murder go hand in hand. If something should transpire then it's not a problem—unlike in the city. The village midwife aborts the foetus with her wooden paddle and thread.

Now this is not a problem in the city either. From outside it may be a health centre, clinic for childless women, or maternity home, but inside you can get any treatment for Rs 5000. There it's like a replay of the scene at the time of Baqra Eid—the butchers cutting the throat of one goat and flaying another. One is given an injection, the other is being laid out on a stretcher. A third one is being made to sit up and the social workers are writing her name. Who brings these women, girls, adolescents? I have seen very few coming alone. Most have men with them, the ones who take out the five thousand rupees from their pocket. Some have old women with them. These doctors have also divided up their territories like the local police. Just as you have medicine shops in one locality, carpet shops in another, crockery in a third, in the same way these clinics spread out from the posh areas to the lanes and neighbourhoods, fulfilling a need. Where there is more work there are also more clinics. Some people even have to come every month. Fortunately, now there are injections and minor operations, otherwise this was one more thing for which you had to take out time from your busy day.

In the same way, many aunties take out the time to throw parties for their lively, popular, young nieces, inviting pleasant and cultured people and, by presenting the girls as virgins, get kudos for their thoughtfulness. Many of these aunties, looking at the bodies of mothers who have had several children, put them into school and college uniforms and assuage the slavering lust of men.

But the true character of those who claim to be the Mahmud Ghaznavis of women is a different matter. Either they pass out under the effects of alcohol and Mahlaqa does a bunk with the contents of their pocket, or they try to convince her that their powers only failed them under the spell of her beauty, otherwise during their lifetime they have given women such a good time that they go about touching their ears, begging for mercy.

Having a good time is the prime occupation of some. Those who bet on race horses have an amazing knack for wheedling out the entire wealth of the household on the promise that when they return there'll be a Rolls Royce standing outside, air conditioners inside, and everyone will be draped in brocade. If they come home dragging their feet, then you must forget it right away—fortunes can change in the twinkling of an eye. Those who take a chance on people and opportunities, as they do on race horses, regard people also as money that can slip through the fingers and suddenly change into something else. The wife also seems like a race horse, and life too—take a bet on it for ten rupees.

I rattled the chains of morality which says that income from betting on races is immoral. But on the contrary I was taunted as a fanatic, backward and traditional, while the race horses continued to gallop with a vengeance. In the house where I lived the earnings from race horses was used to pay for feasts for Quran *khatms* and for fulfilling the obligation to donate *deghs* of *biryani* at the anniversaries of saints. To pray for victory for the race horses, trips were made to Data Sahib and prayers were said standing on one leg.

I was the mistress of the house. It was a love marriage. But when I would come home from the office, I would see eight to ten American and Christian girls having tea in my house. When I was coming and going from my office, I would spot the same girls roaming around with my husband in his car, or standing chatting with him on the rooftop of the office. If I threw a fit or objected, I would be told in a sarcastic voice: 'You are mad. You've gone crazy. That girl is really sweet; one keeps bumping into such girls. You are just a wife.'

'You are just a wife.' For every crisis this was the response I got. Money is being embezzled from the office and being spent on a good time with women. The whole world is saying: 'What kind of a wife are you? Why don't you check him?' And if you remonstrate with him pat comes the answer 'What's it to you what I do? If you were such a goody-goody you should have married a maulvi!'

How can girls finish off a love marriage behind curtains of silence? But then the secrets came out. Now he was faced with the prospect of losing his job, and prison bars. The same wife who was not supposed to interfere in his morals was being treated as a mentor. Beseeching, imploring, swearing to keep to his word, praising her faithfulness; begging her to go to the Secretary and senior officials and to have the matter closed.

The scene changes. Everything is sorted out. Now the same secretary, or officer, and the wife who had come in handy in remedying the situation are the villains. Then the scene changes again—the pieces on the board change. There is a new board. Once again the king is about to be checkmated but the pawn comes in handy. But the pawn is only a pawn; the king is a king after all.

Night falls. The glasses overflow. The night prolongs. Four-letter words slip out and begin to reverberate in the rooms. The verandah is arrayed with vomit of many hues. Verses begin to spout from faltering lips—but the one who is the poet is inside her room with her kids and a book. Those who claim not to be poets are drowning in poetry. Dead drunk, he stumbles to the bedroom. The next instant he is asleep and snoring. 'Forget it, let bygones be bygones.'

The sound of ankle bells, dancers plucking off the rupee notes held against their cheeks...a *mujra*...sitting on laps and making others sit on yours...paying homage to manhood... my sitting and listening to the mujra, forced to put up with it, but worried about the kids being neglected and, seeing their father's daily preoccupations, following in the same footsteps—God forbid!

The phone rings in the middle of the night—it's from the police station—so and so has been hauled up for making a public nuisance of himself. Come and bail him out. You pay up. The next day the same person will be heard saying: 'Don't talk about her *yaar*. Keep your mouth shut. She is the wife of a friend, but what can I say...Enough!'

To drown out the stress of a full day's work and the irritations of the evening, I thought, let me also have a taste. I picked up a glass of wine—at once the flame of honour flared up. How can a woman compete with a man? Are you trying to vie with me? In whose company have you acquired this bad habit? Who is the lucky man? It is broadcast to the whole world and sets off the fingers wagging of those progressives who raise slogans for women's equality in the name of revolution. Morality is only needed by women. If a man appears on television then he is accomplished—if a woman does then she is a loose character, a publicity hound. If a man has the opportunity just of making a peep on the radio it is considered a great honour but if a woman participates in any programme it is held to be an excuse for having a good time. For a man to go off every now and then in the evenings for dinners without intimation is a necessity and for the woman to go to official functions, even after intimation, is to flout his marital rights. For a man to stay away from the house without notice is part of his freedom. For a woman to announce her going on her own for some work, or meeting, is held to be unbridled freedom.

In the West such attitudes among men have prompted women to become lesbians so that the bruises and vexations would be reduced. But when I look at a lesbian I feel uneasy. I remember a woman critic who was well known for such inclinations. She had even kept a dog for her safety. Every man wanted to discover the secret of her habits. One day I found the bell around my neck: I had to go through the test of spending the night at her house. It was the end of summer but out of fear I chose to sleep in the courtyard. The lady would get up now and then, swallow some pills, or drink water, then come and sit on my bed. I would be cursing the instigators of the test. I was lying there tightly curled up, fearful, when she poured perfume on her hand and started rubbing my neck and chest. I stopped her. I thought the perfume would make me throw up. I spent the whole night in this dilemma. In the morning I left an unhappy lady and went home.

This lady had never been to the West. Many women who've been to the West and have tasted all kinds of experiences, they too upon coming back either become lesbians or sink into nostalgia and start living in their old environment. One woman had a nervous breakdown after a failed love affair and returned to the country and till today she is a prisoner of the same love and the same environment. The men are in the same boat. They go on a trip, see a girl, fall in love; the wife immediately begins to seem dispensable. If the Western girl gives them a shove then for the rest of their life they will keep her locks in an envelope and keep showing it to people. If they see a girl in a window then for the rest of their life they will be spouting poetry, short stories, love stories, while waiting for another scene to appear at the window. However, the Eastern man is very domesticated. In every love affair he proposes marriage, is ready to settle the dower. To save the affair from scandal he's learnt to refer to her as 'sister' from the films and this is still a tried and tested formula.

Experts in psychology (who are mostly male) see these men as mother's boys, who keep searching for their mothers in their lovers, wives, and friends. They are aware of their unfulfilled personalities and are prey to feelings of inferiority. But because of their argumentative nature, obstinacy, and unreasonableness, they make it their life's mission to keep doing something. They feel a sense of achievement in hurting someone else's ego. This unreasonableness and argumentativeness is also a reflection of the philosophy of love and hate which holds that if psychiatric patients receive love then they withdraw but if there is hatred and tension then they are all over you.

I was on this see-saw of life. But because of the immoral behaviour around me my inner self had prepared its own moral compass to which I myself would be answerable. My inner self, to extricate itself from crises, prepared its own rules of procedure. This can take two shapes—one to start the journey internally and become one of those women who go and sit in graveyards and tombs of *pirs* and prostrate themselves the whole day at Data Sahib. But this was shameful for the blood that coursed through my veins. The other way was to talk to myself and write. This proved to be a true companion, stronger than a blood relationship, closer than my children. Rather, the problem of children was a unique one for me: all men in the house, and I the lone woman.

The children—and that too the younger child—poked fun at my being the only woman thus: 'Mother, everyone is male in this house, including the dog. You are the only woman. How can you compete with us?'

This and other quips would be said in jest and all the men would enjoy it and laugh. If I was angry at the kids their father would say: 'The children will behave the way you behave.' Getting encouragement they would become even bolder in opposing me. Under the constant influence of their father's family, living on the winnings from the races influenced the children's behaviour. Who could explain to them that there is a difference between an honest income and the income from races? Little by little their ideals changed. Their father and other relatives became their heroes. Everyone relished racy stories while I wanted to keep a lid on such matters. By and by the mother was termed 'undesirable' and the need to find fault with her grew stronger. Because reading and writing were not acceptable, so the mother also was unacceptable and egging them on was this feeling of superiority: Who does mother think she is? We'll humiliate her and look brave in the eyes of all the relatives. We'll be heroes and have our own identity. In other words, getting respect through studying and learning was looked down upon and thus, the balance of life was weighted with one more rock of hatred.

My writing offered a shield in front of all these hatreds. My pen made a dam to hold back the flood. A house came up inside the house. My own house, the house of dialogue between me and my self, in which pen and paper became my friends to console me and make me smile. I began to rely so much on their friendship that the day I didn't read I felt empty. And all alone.

I like being alone. On the one hand the whole world knows that I grace *mehfils*, and on the other hand, all alone, for half and hour or one hour every day, in seclusion and silence, I race against my thoughts, I laugh, I smile, and like a mad person I talk to myself. I love talking to myself. Good and bad thoughts, both, echo inside me and come to life. The bad thoughts batter my mind and heart and the good thoughts make me laugh heartily all by myself. Because of these habits some people say that I am egotistic; narcissistic; I don't love anyone as much as myself; I don't allow any relationship to take precedence over me; I get more pleasure out of poetry than from being a woman, wife, or mother. It's poetry that calms the turmoil, fears, and convulsions of my mind. But why do I forget whose branches have helped my poetry to climb? No matter how stubborn, obstinate or rebellious I was, if the personality opposing me had not been weak or flexible, then my growing tendrils would have developed within social limits. If, instead of accepting the boldness of my spirit, I had been chained down then what? Even then I knew how to keep myself going. The reason for this is that the power of mental discipline inside me is like having Hercules in my grasp. I would say that this has been the case since the time I used to say my Tahajjud prayers and *jalali wazifas*. I used to test myself by saying: 'God, wake me up at 4 in the morning.' I wouldn't put on the alarm clock but at exactly 4 o'clock my eyes would open. After that whenever any project, work, or responsibility came before me I would make a decision, commit myself to it, pray, and despite other matters on my mind I would make a plan. Start the work and use whatever time I got. Such moments came few and far between in my life when I would say oh, how I have wasted my time. Because of my ability to make the most of my time, along with the rest of the world, I myself would wonder how everything manages to get done. These activities include recreation, meeting friends, and those mehfils too which some people consider to be the be-all and end-all of my life and work.

Success has not been the single refrain in my life. I failed in class five: in one subject I got full marks and in another zero. In one of the debating competitions at university too I lost. At work because I didn't suck up I was demoted several times. I never asked why, nor was I told. It also happened once that I got promoted. I was to take up the charge of the department but two of the employees kicked up a fuss. Their reasoning was that a woman can't be head of the department. They went around the offices with resolutions. I was not posted there but after a few days on my insistence the posting went ahead. When I went to the rooms of the two gentlemen who had opposed me their opposition evaporated. Thus the way was paved for a woman to become an officer.

'Decent women should not leave the house.' This phrase is the motto of men of all ages, ranks, and looks. Wives who are bold, unscrupulous, and headstrong are stopped by using another excuse. They say: 'I'll take you myself.' But there are many places where the husband is not invited. There the wife has to cajole him repeatedly: '*Arre*, they insisted that you should come.' Then, upon seeing the husband, the same people begin to pass comments as they would have done had he not come, saying things like 'Oh, her husband is such a bore!'

Some husbands wave the fact of being the husband like a flag over their head. Tied to her like the tail of a paper kite, they accompany her to every city, every function, every country; or else the wife has to stay at home like a tethered cow. There is also another way of preventing the wife from going anywhere—killing the snake without breaking the stick. You tell him: 'We have to go to such and such a place.' The reply: 'Yes, we'll go.' Then silence. At the appointed time both get ready but that's all. At last the wife gets fed up and asks: 'Aren't we going?' He replies 'Where?' Very patiently: 'Didn't we have to go to such and such a place today?' 'Oh, no, I am not going there, I'm going somewhere else.' In a sulk, the wife flings her handbag to one side and her sari to the other and lies down. At once with a long deep sigh the husband calls out: 'Ok then I'm off.'

Later on she finds out that he did go there after all. But when she confronts him he retorts: 'I felt like it so I went. If you had wanted you could have gone too.'

If this phrase keeps being hammered at you then one day the dam of patience bursts and then in such houses the conversation and relationship is reduced to this: 'I am going', or sometimes even this is unnecessary. Many houses in one house. Each indifferent to the other, strangers, content to hurt each other emotionally; prosperous, contented, fortunate households held up as examples.

It also happens sometimes that the role assumed by the husband is also assumed by the wife. The husband can't leave the house without the wife's say-so. She may not make him grind spices like Hasrat Mohani's wife but she does harass him in the same way. These husbands stop meeting their friends. Even at the office they are working for the wife's pleasure all the time. They meet the wife's relatives. They make copies of her manuscripts. They cook for her. All she has to do is to sit dolled up. They do everything—from stitching the falls of her saris to changing the baby's nappies and preparing its milk—and are quite content.

If you think of friendship then there isn't any such thing between a husband and wife. If you address him informally he himself gets embarrassed and says: '*I* don't say anything, it's the parents who tell me: "Your wife doesn't respect you. She calls you by your name".' They keep on telling the wife: 'Don't talk nonsense,' but if the wife says the same thing it's an affront to their manhood. A man may strike a woman to his heart's content but if the wife raises her hand in retaliation this is an insult to his manhood and is regarded as exceeding the limits for the wife. Then discussions on the extent to which a wife can be beaten and on which parts of her body, as allowed by Shariah, reinforce such ideas.

Reflection—this is a strange word and a river as well. If I go back over its journey I find myself at the age of five. When my mother told me to grind the spices I went out into the lane and asked my peers: 'Is she my real mother?' I go a little further to when I was seven—made to wear a burqa—I would keep stumbling; 13—stopped from meeting all male cousins—ordered to cover my chest with the dupatta—protest—cry in the wilderness; 15—hunger strike for admission into college; 19—making a fuss to enter into university; 20—insisting on a marriage of my own choice—but what a year, what a marriage—my thoughts became my jailors. My mentors and heroes were also the kind of people who would go to jail, write verses, and talk about the poor. And then the kind of job I got working in the villages—as though at the core of my being was the zest for a simple life. This zest kept me away from many other tastes: wealth, jewellery, clothes, pomp and show—and hunger. If I call it greed it will be even clearer. I have seen people with well-filled and protruding stomachs quivering in front of food, their mouths watering. I have seen frustrated men who have not known love lose their senses in front of a female, trembling with the longing to look into her eyes and unburden their souls. I have seen the well-dressed dying with the desire that if only God had given them more than one body they could fulfil their longing to wear more and more new clothes. I have seen the rich saving their money and wandering around in rags so that when they died even the shroud that was put over them was borrowed; and their children fighting like donkeys to take possession of their bodies, so that the one who fulfilled the obligations of burial would be able to reap the rewards of his good work (God have mercy on us!) and take possession of the property.

But perhaps—and the reason for this was my approach rather than self-analysis and self-awareness—I was rejecting all that was happening before me to show displeasure and to distance myself from it; declaring that I would not participate in it. Perhaps it was also fashionable to keep oneself aloof—but why adopt this fashion alone? Why not any other?

The explanation for this is clear to some extent and to some extent unknown. In the whole household there is only one person who is a writer or poet. In the house of the distinguished poet or writer literature is an unknown word. The same gift which appeared in the garb of a poetic nature bestowed upon me the gift of asceticism and contentment so that even in solitude I feel refreshed by its fragrance. Because of this asceticism and contentment, I learnt both in life and at work to look everyone in the eye and talk boldly and, seeing the compulsions of those who were less self-aware than me, thanking God that I didn't acquire the practice of expressing myself only by losing control of myself. Instead of counting out my future in bundles of notes, I searched for it in the patterns of words which could bear witness for coming generations.

But this idea too was wrong that a woman could not talk openly nor could a man think of a woman except in terms of sex. So what happened? Mysteries should be allowed to remain mysteries; even then the innocence of nature becomes apparent but when mysteries are dressed in lies then to save yourself you have to concoct stories: 'So and so called and he was very solicitous.' 'She was sitting with so and so.' 'She was standing with so and so.'

At work someone said: 'She's turned from a peon into an officer!' The officers said: 'She is headstrong, she must have connections.' The newspapers wrote whatever they wanted.

Because I didn't spend clandestine evenings with journalists in hotels nor did I praise their half-baked writings, so naturally it made me bad—a bad woman.

Let alone my enemies, even my friends verify my being bad. Someone's wife asked her husband: 'Where do you stay the whole day? Do you even spare a thought for all that goes on in the house? And these kids born of our reckless nights, they are yours after all.' Then that's it. For opening her mouth the poor woman gets taunted: 'What a quick tongue! Looks like you are meeting.... I am warning you!'

The amazing thing is that having said this to his wife, he turns to me approvingly: 'What a strong woman you are! You can sort out even the high and mighty. You are my heroine.' Seeing the grace of God on both sides, in my heart of hearts, I laugh.

One friend became renowned as a revolutionary for writing about the oppression of women but his own wife couldn't come and go freely; if she went anywhere she had to be accompanied or she couldn't leave the house. If you confronted him he would say: '*I* don't say anything, it's my father who doesn't like it.'

Another friend, having written moving columns on the oppression of women and turned himself into a Rashidul Khairi, when it came to the question of his own wife's employment, dramatically announced: 'If you are going to office then I should take leave. After all what's going to happen to the children?' When he himself is away from the house day and night then it's curtains to watching over the children. But yes, if the wife goes to work to earn money, then home, honour, dishonour, the world, and the scandals of working women all raise their heads.

'Are you going to such and such a function? Take me along.'

'All right. Be ready.'

I arrive at his house. The wife is at the door with a sarcastic smile. 'Where all do you roam around with my husband in tow? It's just women that don't appeal to you, it seems. I too like to go out, you know.'

The husband stands there blushing away, giggling. He doesn't clarify that he had rung up himself to invite me. I laugh in response. I am furious but I can't say anything. The Laloka who is called sharp-tongued is laughing. The Laloka who lives among beasts is listening. What else can she do?

NOTE

1. The neighbour is referring to her husband. Many married women of the old school never utter their husband's name.

Chapter Eight
At Meera Bai's Feet

B.F. Skinner, the most well-known authority on psychology after Freud, rejected fame and freedom both as illusions. In the same connection the photographer Richard Avedon, in his autobiography, talks about the vanishing of mirages. Someone commenting on my verses once said: 'Kishwar Naheed's poetry is riddled with love'. That got me thinking. I have stayed away from that prettified, coy love which goes about twisting dupattas between its teeth. My early poetry has traditional love but for traditional poetry love is not necessary. In this traditional poetry my only companion has been woman: a woman's consciousness and voice. My early poetry which can be called romantic poetry dates back entirely to my college years. Fortunately I destroyed it myself, otherwise future critics would have held them up as being representative of it.

In my childhood I listened to mushairas till late into the night—in Bulandshahr at the mushairas held around the new moon, and in Aligarh sitting on Mother's lap behind the blinds. The one thing we brothers and sisters were allowed to do was indulge in *bait baazee*. To the extent that while dyeing dupattas, crimping the dyed dupattas with our hands or the lids of pots, drying dupattas, breaking vermicelli into shorter lengths, drying vermicelli, preparing vegetables, kneading dough, weaving *niwar* beds and tightening the tape, in every situation, we would carry on with our bait baazee. The amazing thing was that rather than the ancient or classical poets there would be a greater preponderance of verses by modern poets. We got these verses from two sources: one was that all the young men returning from Aligarh would be enthusiastically reciting the verses of Majaz, Shakeel, Jagannath Azad, Jigar, and Hafeez and would especially be getting the girls to memorize the poems of Ihsan Danish:

'*Beetay huway kuch din aisey hain tanhaiyee jinhen duhratee hai*' (Of bygone days some live again in solitude), or '*Mazdoor ki baitee ki rukhsati*' (The departure of the labourer's daughter), or Majaz's poem '*Ai gham-e-dil kiya karun, ai wahshat-e-dil kiya karun*' (Oh sorrowing heart what shall I do? Oh desolate heart what shall I do?). Furthermore, everything that was read at mushairas during the industrial exhibitions in Meerut, Aligarh, and Bulandshahr would be preserved in the notebooks of every girl or would be on her lips with the same intonation. Using melodic tones to utter verses whether at home or in the women's gatherings of the Muslim League was not frowned upon. But yes, for a woman to write poetry, or to think as a woman, was a sin which had not been committed by anyone.

Why did I start thinking in this serious way at such a young age and why did the classical element predominate in my poetry? If I analyse this myself then I see around me the halo of those elders who were more than 30 years older than me. I grew up in their shadow as a friend, understanding their poetry, writing poetry, playing with words. The manner of giving respect to elders, awareness of the history and culture of the language, depth of thought, all this was their gift to me. When I went to Dhaka, one of my elders upon seeing me said at once: 'Tell me frankly, whose are these verses? For poetic language to be as developed at this age is quite unusual.'

I was once reading a ghazal at a mushaira on the radio when a senior poet congratulated me and had me repeat the verse several times. Whenever I went to his house to get him to explain a verse or word, he remembered that day with great pleasure. There was one elder who, whenever I asked for his permission to try out a particular word in a verse, would on the one hand, shower me with a thousand blessings, and on the other, show me through verses in Urdu, Persian, Arabic, and Hindi the versatility of the word and its wide range of meanings. There was another elder from whom I wanted to learn Persian; months went by in explaining each verse. The art and philosophy of composition were garbs of poetry and life which would never come to an end.

In those days such talented and accomplished writers were associated with radio and television that it was daunting to send in a piece of writing. If the piece was good you would get a lot of affection and blessings. It would be mentioned proudly in front of others and you would feel encouraged. If the piece was even slightly below the mark you would get such a shouting that you would remember it forever. You would be told something like: 'The schools will have to refund your past and future fees.' Or you would have to listen to the taunt: 'Was this what the schools prepared you for that you should write such bad verses or such faulty prose?' It was such gracious teachers who taught me the difference between *hamd* and *naat*, who introduced me to the finer points of what you could and could not do in composing the rhymes of ghazals, who encouraged me to experiment with freshness and fluidity in language; and who, to help me find my individual style, told me which of the contemporary and classical native and foreign writers I should be reading. Rather like school homework, they gave me their work to read analytically. They advised me to write long poems. In fact, many times I would be ordered to shut myself up in a room and not come out until I had written something. They also taught me the skill of speaking on the radio. Mother had already laid the foundation for modulating words by teaching me to recite the Quran. It was the 'golden voices' of the radio who knew how to use words, who dressed these foundations with cultural awareness.

One more clarification as to what was the cause of my friendship and closeness to those who were 40 years older than me. If I think about it then the reason was that none of my peers had got married by then. They were not friendly with poets and writers; they only knew some by face. The girls of my age were in final year and boys of my husband's age were still hunting for jobs. During my college years I stayed in an area where, through the elderly Ustad Soofi Sahib, I got to know the senior poets of the city, rather of the country. I met them, heard their verses, listened to the discussions on poetry, and was introduced to the manners and customs of a literary and cultural Lahore. I met those personalities who are now part of history and then it moved on from there. As I became known in the world of poetry and literature I forged links with my peers, and then a day came when the elders started accusing me of ignoring them and turning away from them.

Like the Czechoslovakian poet Seifert I say and remember: 'I have a window/A beautiful spring day sparkles before it/I have a dog/Which looks with human eyes/And a blue notebook/In which are bound the beautiful names of people.'

What was the reason for turning away from them? The same which confronts everyone in life. Those people who are your friends are so close and dear that others appear like strangers, unknown and at a distance. Reassess this after a gap of five to six years; the scene changes. New names, new faces, and a new environment surround you. People stay the same, stay where they were, but you change and your temperament changes. And the seasons of intimacy wane into the winter of distance. Yes, in my youth, having done the course of Adeeb Fazil, the solid traditions of poetry and literature had become absorbed into my nature.

I wasn't given books to read but whenever and from wherever I got them I would devour them hungrily. Anna Akhmatova would always have by her pillow Pushkin, the Bible, Shakespeare, and Dostoyevsky. I would keep even literary works hidden in between my course books by my pillow to read.

Thus, I often regret not having read Nasim Hijazi or Tirathram Firozpuri, and that I couldn't find the time to read the acclaimed novelists of my era. But even while having children, I read *Iblis ki Majlis-e-Shoora* and the work of Qurratul Ain Tahira in detail and got satisfaction out of it.

Thanks to my elders, I watched mujras by the senior singers of today. The mujras of olden days were not those where people were teased or there was obscene behaviour. The singer was paid beforehand. All the guests would be seated on the floor, or on a white sheet, and as the night progressed the beauty of the singer's voice would set alight the varied verses of the classical poets. The session would conclude with the morning call to prayer. *Payas* and *nihari* would be eaten and it was from here that people would set off for their homes and, at times, for their offices.

I was also able, thanks to these elders, to go to the Shahi Mohalla in the afternoon and listen to the singing. This was a unique and distinct culture but I had been frightened off from this area. Despite going there several times during the day no one was willing to take me there in the evenings (what the atmosphere was like in the evenings, I will keep for another occasion).

Following in the footsteps of the elders and the books and dictionaries they had in their homes I too built up a library. Subsequently, running the official libraries of many departments I learnt how to catalogue books and arrange them according to subject.

In the process of learning from the gatherings and discussions that took place in the houses of the elders, an important role was played by those organizations that had weekly meetings, whether these meetings took place in Nisbet Road or at the YMCA. At that time I didn't even realize that the philosophies of the two associations were opposed to each other. My links with people were also along the same lines. I wanted to learn from every writer who was older than me. I was a frightened bird in a locked cage. I was so fond of reading that I even enjoyed reading the paper of the packets in which the groceries came. Similarly, when stirring the pot, going through files at the office, returning to the house by tonga or bus, whenever a line of verse, couplet, title of a poem, or stanza came to me I would write it down. After that if I didn't have the time to write, my mind would be suffused by the fragrance of that one line. It would keep going round and round in my head. My hands would be busy with other things—cooking the rotis, washing the dishes, washing the clothes, wiping the floor, getting through all the housework. In the afternoon if I had any time to myself or left over from the housework, at once I would take some paper out and start writing; which is why most of my poems and ghazals are from one sitting.

In my first two books there are many resonances of contemporary poets who were senior to me. Especially in the poems, despite all my efforts, I could not escape from the influence of Rashid Sahib and Mukhtar Siddiqui Sahib. Nevertheless, the themes of these poems were according to my own taste while the influence of these two gentlemen is quite apparent in the style. It was these two gentlemen, in fact, who encouraged me to write poems. Mukhtar Sahib had even written down a stanza from my poem in his diary, perhaps to give me encouragement. My contemporaries tried to draw conclusions from this but why should it have been so remarkable? There was nothing unusual about this: '*Bila kashan muhabbat pe jo huwa so huwa*' (If it happened in love without suffering, so be it).

My relations with the literati and my peers was not on a one-to-one basis. The two of us—Yusuf and I—always went everywhere together and the meetings were also together. In the office environment and preoccupations there was hardly any time for starting literary discussions. A few friends here and there referred books to me and gave me guidance. Otherwise, I would go to the shops and buy the latest books; borrow books from the library; or get acquainted with books and recipients of literary prizes by reading the reviews published in English journals from abroad. Even then I have read very little. My knowledge is very limited and I feel it. My only consolation is that because of the Persian I studied in childhood and the guidance afterwards of teachers, I read the Persian poets and subsequently collected the works of the new Farsi poets and tried to understand the language and tone. Which is why I could be true to the poetic traditions of the ghazal to some extent.

The ability to make poetry and other artistic endeavours speak with a singular voice was something which was handed down to me by the traditions of my venerable masters. For this reason, in the circles of my friends, among the singers, painters, people associated with the film industry, stars of theatre and dance, and those who had a love for language, all those people are also included who always wore hand-woven cloth, who worked in the villages, and adopted the ascetic traditions in which showing off is frowned upon.

I also translated literature and works in other languages. In the beginning I translated poetry and stories for children at the rate of a rupee per page. At one time I did translations to earn money. But my dream of making money could not be fulfilled because those who commissioned the translations disappeared. I became inclined to do translations on my own after having done the book of my own poems. Ezra Pound said that through translation you also become aware of the complexities of your own language. While translating I have to pass through the process of 'transcreation'. I have translated a lot, both prose and poetry, and during my period as editor of *Mah-e-Nau* I persuaded many writers to translate modern foreign writers.

During martial law when even words were in chains, we had no other option apart from translation. Clothing the anger of Palestinian writers and the call to arms of African writers in our own words, we would feel satisfied that we had got across some message at least to the masses, e.g. '*Habs key alim mein parandey bhi mar jatey hain*' (During humidity even birds die) is a Hadith but so long as we didn't stamp it with the word 'Hadith' it could not be published. The censors censored essays, names, even Quranic verses.

During the same martial law period, along with other Pakistani writers, my poems too were translated into other languages. In Canada the translator was awarded a prize by Columbia University and the woman who translated them in London was invited by The Women's Press to publish a book.

It was during this period that while travelling abroad I met many important writers and they were thus introduced to Pakistani literature. In fact, in many places this turned out to be their first introduction to Pakistan as well because in libraries throughout the world, in the section relating to the subcontinent, you could find my writings. But in the Urdu section there are only a few worthwhile books here and there.

During every foreign trip it had to be emphasized that we people were not living in the Stone Age. In those days *Chador aur Char Diwari*' (the veil and four walls of the house) was getting a great deal of publicity. All the diplomatic staff were also involved in this propaganda. To convey the struggle of Pakistani women in writing and in their daily life to foreigners is a task that tries your patience because they are convinced that we are ignorant women who sit at home.

The group of writers, artists, painters, and singers who were my friends opened new vistas for me and led my poetic experimentation down new paths which, in the manner of Ghalib, would only be grasped by future generations. While putting my experiences into words I was taken to pieces so many times and attacked with all kinds of comments such as: 'You don't get great literature from turning a diary into poetry'. What do I care about great literature? And what makes you think that your commendation will turn it into great literature? Yesterday's braggarts are nowhere to be found in the journals of today. Go and write something yourself; you can't fire a cannon by letting off hot air! One writer has been sitting on a cannon for 35 years firing off books. Whoever doesn't acknowledge his status is struck off the list of writers through his pen.

A strange and pleasing thing is that from 1960 till today both at home and abroad, women writers, from Simone de Beauvoir to Erica Jong and Toni Morrison, have established themselves on the literary scene. They have discussed the various aspects of the male–female relationship in their writing and challenged the nuclear family and the supremacy of men. The way women themselves have written about the treatment of women's bodies in the country came in for criticism but it is a truth that shouts from the rooftops. Women's writings changed the entire literary landscape. Otherwise they were only restricted to writing about their psychological confusions and poetry such as '*Jahan Rehana Rehti Thi*' or '*Meray Handam, Meray Dost*'. Revolution, poetry, life, relationships, contradictions—the perseverance of women writers has been useful in bringing all these experiences to the sphere of poetry. In Pakistan also many travelogues, influenced by the work of women writers, have been able to encompass and throw light on human relationships.

Putting the behaviour of writers to one side, if you ask anyone 'Have you heard such and such a woman's story?', the answer you'll get: 'What story? We went to look at her low neck!' Ask someone: 'Did you hear so and so's poem?' The answer will be: 'I don't know about the poem. But I do like her bare arms!' Ask someone: 'Did you hear so and so's essay?' You'll get the reply: 'The essay can go to hell! What I like is to accompany her home. She smiles throughout the journey. She feels very shy in front of me, no doubt she's got the hint.' You ask: 'Isn't she someone's wife?' The reply: 'Perhaps, but if she was good why would she leave the house at all?'

I have come across many travellers on the literary road and learnt something from most. From one grace in speaking, from another dignity in conversation; from one simplicity and spontaneity in the company of words; from another the advice to keep studying the classics. From one the skill of going over the many nuances of a word in solitude; from another the candour of silence; or the impact of understatement—all this I learnt from my elders.

Those who were younger than me also taught me: keep filling the cup of self-confidence, you'll always find it empty. They explained to me: 'Don't count writers as your friends, get to grips with their art. Don't get close to them, otherwise your art will lose its lustre.' They cautioned me: 'Don't do a good deed to someone else for the sake of reward; always expect enmity in return.'

But the trouble is you can't do without others. Even in death you need someone else to close your eyes. You must have some hook or the other to hang your relationships on. After writing each poem or ghazal I showed it to my family since the heart wants to share such things. But each poem and ghazal would be held to be a reflection of some domestic incident and thus unpublishable. I was so disheartened that I adopted the same behaviour as in my mother's house: writing ghazals when no one was looking and hiding them in my drawer in the office. When the book was published then everyone at home would read the poems and ghazals like everyone else.

Every time I put a book together I got sick. All those moments which appeared in the form of poems on various occasions, when you go through them as a collection then the sense of grief hits you so hard that you almost keel over. This has always been the dialogue between my doctor and myself. The poor doctors have got their certificates by studying the science of the body. The science of the mind is beyond them.

The birth of every poem is at one and the same time a moment of peace as well as of torment. I had to go through so many trials and tribulations while writing a poem that each word would manifest itself as a tribute to my being. After finishing a poem I would feel washed, fresh, light, refreshed as though I had woken after a sleep of many nights. As though I had eaten after fasting for many days. Every book has been like giving birth.

Why is political activism and political thought so apparent in my consciousness and my training? The origins of this go back to that time when I learnt to identify things. We used to play gulli danda; I was in the middle of two brothers which is why I used to only play boys' games. I never played with dolls in my childhood. The same stick that was used to hit the gulli would become our flag and all of us kids would chant slogans, take out processions, and have meetings. Partition was just one of a series of political crises. When we came to Pakistan, for example, there was the Korean boom and foreign goods started flowing into the country; the Suez Canal was attacked and we college girls took out processions, weeping and writing poems when Nasser resigned; protesting against 'Thank You America' and PL480; Vietnam; the Chinese Cultural Revolution and the greatest tragedy, the fall of East Pakistan and after that—life brought us face to face with what even our ancestors would not have faced in the *jahilliya*—the Age of Ignorance: lashes, hangings, punishments, censorship, restrictions. Look at our sense of fellow-feeling: Bhutto was hanged on 4 April by Ziaul Haq and on 10 April our leading lights were at the writers' conference convened by this butcher. How can we vouch for the weight of words? We can't even vouch for our own characters!

Anyhow, all these goings on are swimming like poison in my blood. In my country along with women, men are also oppressed: 87 per cent of the country's entire land is under the control of only 13 per cent of the population in the shape of the feudals. The peasants of my country, the earners of all the foreign exchange, are rotting in a 400-year-old environment. And those that barter away their interests make merry in the assemblies and in air-conditioned houses. In my country woman has no identity, she is identified by her relationships with others—she is a sister, wife, mother, daughter—but is she anything on her own?

After the publication of each of my books, especially those on the subject of women, burqa-clad women came to talk to me and seek my advice. Young people have honoured me by involving me in decisions to do with their marriages and careers. However, many women college professors criticized several of my poems, such as 'Farewell to Uterus' and termed them obscene. If anyone asked them: 'You have only read the title. Have you read the poem too?', they were met with the reply: 'After reading the title I didn't dare go any further'. In exactly the same way even till today people blush when reading *Terhi Lakir* and *Lihaf*, and in the same way too they place Amrita Pritam, Kamala Das, and Erica Jong beside the pillar of pornography.

I am keen to read the literature of all my country's languages and I got the opportunity of observing the traditions of these areas at close quarters, which is why if the occasion is to commemorate Shah Latif or Sultan Bahu it is an honour for me to be included among the eulogists. The fire of their writing inspires me to follow in their footsteps because through the voices of honest women these writers have always challenged tyrants. There is no match for the way Anna Akhmatova challenged the dictatorship of her time. Because of her poetry her son had to go through the tribulations of prison—and that too the prison of Stalin's time. To divorce your husband was unusual at that time and in that society. But fed up, she got a divorce and still kept the crown of poetry intact. In spite of assimilating all these soul-racking days and nights her poetry has the freshness of morning. She asks for love, peace, and freedom for people in her poetry.

Similarly, Marina Tsvetaeva compared her life with that of the important historical male and female figures and went on writing poetry saying that revolutionaries are not nurtured; they come up by themselves to answer the questions of their age.

In my poetic journey Pasternak, Mayakovsky and Osip Mendelstam reassured me that 'Poetry is not another name for fulfilment. Let your poems absorb the truth in the same way as truth absorbs everything.' They said: 'Ask those who are fearful of poetry: "Have snakes ever hidden among roses?"'

All my intellectual mentors and senior professors put their hands on my shoulder and gave me very valuable advice which guides me and helps me till today: 'Whatever you are writing and whatever you are doing will meet with much criticism. If you fall into the trap of defending yourself then you won't be able to do anything else for the rest of your life. Water your art diligently for at least 10 years without looking for praise. Then no force in the world will be able to ignore you.'

Poetry gave me much pain. Had I abandoned it perhaps I would have been accepted as a good wife. I would have got the distinction of being a devoted mother; I would have come even closer to my brothers and sisters. But I would also have understood the world less, been less truthful, would have made fewer enemies, and would have found less pleasure in solitude.

Poetry gave me many comforts. The whole country and the whole world seems to be my home. It gave me so many friends and well-wishers that the warmth of love keeps my nose to the grindstone. Poetry gave me such companionship that I am draped with the mantle of affection from head to toe.

It was poetry that melted the glacier of suffering inside me. Vicky Yance started writing at the age of 35 because prior to that she didn't even know how to read and write. There is no comma, no full stop in her writing. Her words give the impression of being hammered into place like stones, a solid wall of words. When I started writing it was exactly like Vicky Yance. This writing was not unique like hers, but this I know that when I got down to writing about the experience I had thought about for ten years, one day and one night were enough. One day for a thousand nights—one night for one thousand nights. Rhymes making up a style...the way poets are. About which Auden said that for a poet whose style cannot be described you can either repeat it as an example or you can make an ugly imitation of it.

Chapter Nine
The Birth of Yashodhara

In his researches the British psychologist Douglas recounts the stories of those women who used to make a pact with the devil. Among these stories is the one about the husband in one unhappy family who vomits when he returns home and discovers that he has thrown up a dog's paw and a child's fingers. He also refers to the spirits in the confessional statements of the seventeenth century who would wander about in the guise of wolves and butterflies and would be fully equipped to fight with the devil.

These things come to mind when I think about my birth and my life's journey. Truly, my birth was no big deal or moment of joy for the house—I was the fifth-born and a girl. Given the physical needs of men and women, for a child to be born every one and a half years, or one year and nine months, was an accepted fact. This was a period when no one knew how babies were born, or how they were prevented. One morning the cry of a mewling infant from the courtyard would announce to all that there was a new arrival, and the whole house would get a taste of the caudle made from dried ginger and the semolina halwa.

Most of us brothers and sisters took after our father's family: short and dark, with narrow foreheads, small eyes, and small hands and feet. This has a bearing on the story that follows.

A king begged of the sun that it should rise every morning to wake up his wife, and the sun abides by this custom till today: it bestows the rank of princess on every girl when she wakes up. From childhood till old age, whenever I would think of myself as a princess, there were many benefactors who would call me an un-fairytale-like character and force me to confront myself. This is not self-pity but rather it is like Jacques Roubaud's Princess Hoppy who is much loved and who also falls victim to many conspiracies; who devises the names and punishments of her abductors and who admits at the end: 'Don't believe in stories because stories just lead to other stories.'

Typhoid really made a mess of whatever looks I had. It hounded me for a long time. I had typhoid four times between the ages of five and seven. Then three times between the ages of 12 and 14. My body would turn from yellow to white. My palate would start feeling like rubber from eating sago. My forehead was narrow to start with; my complexion became even darker, a muddy slate colour. My features were rough and mismatched. Scrawny, dark, with long pigtails, my photograph would look as scary as I did myself. It was common in those days to have a pet name that was different from ones proper name. Mine was 'Chuttoo'. One of my brothers was called 'Nosha', one was 'Dulha', and one was 'Acchan'. Among the sisters only one was called 'Billo'. This was a custom not only in UP but also in Punjab. Yusuf's nickname was 'Kaka' and I also kept nicknames for my children—'Mizo' and 'Fichu'. In fact Mizo became so well-known that few people knew his real name.

My real name was Kishwar Jahan. Until class nine it stayed this way. In those days there would be unusual names in the magazines and two names would be written together. Like the contributors to these magazines I changed my name from Kishwar Jahan to Kishwar Naheed. My other sisters also changed their names in this way. But they never had the opportunity of writing under their own names anywhere. So I was the only one who changed from Chutto to Kishwar Naheed.

After marriage there was much insistence and unpleasantness: 'Change your name, it doesn't look as if you are married.' But I had the solid sceptre of senior women writers in front of me: the majority of them hadn't changed their names. I too was of their tribe.

I turned 12 and a weight descended on my body. I was told to cover myself properly with the dupatta. The newly emerging buds piercing through my kamiz, like pinpricks, were offensive: I had to wear a thick kamiz. And one day all of a sudden stains appeared on my shalwar. Despite reading *Behishti Zevar* I was quite ignorant. I went straight to my older sister in tears and told her what had happened, expressing the fear that perhaps there was a boil inside which had burst. She heard me out and then calmly said: 'It's nothing. It happens with everyone.'

'With you too?' I burst out.

'Yes, yes,' she said taking out some old, torn cloths from a trunk.

I still couldn't believe it. 'Show me,' I said.

'Everyone doesn't get it at the same time!' she snapped.

'Get what? This is the second or third time it has happened. The two times it happened I washed my shalwar. When the stains didn't go I cut them out and sewed up the shalwar again. But it became smaller. I have already cut up two shalwars. How many will I spoil? Oh, my white shalwars!'

Before I could start wailing again, she thrust the remedy in my hands and another painful journey began.

The restrictions on meeting male cousins on narrow staircases and in closed rooms led to other outlets. The obsession with prayers was followed by a keen interest in astrology. The whole night would be spent observing the stars changing their position, sinking, rising, searching for my own star sign. I would read in secret whatever book on astronomy I could lay my hands on. Mother would creep in at night on tiptoe to try and catch me out: she thought it was just another excuse to meet boys. Finding me casting horoscopes would make her furious. I would sit for hours with the Quran. It would make Mother really happy. When she saw me writing something she got suspicious. She asked my sisters to find out. I said I was looking for rhymes. I was thrashed and forbidden to have a notebook by me when reading the Quran. The books on palmistry and astrology were all burnt accompanied by Mother's exclamations: '*Hai*, what could I have eaten to have conceived you?'

Marriage, wedding night, pregnancy, the movements of the baby inside the womb, all these stages came and went without making any waves in my life. The other day when this ordinary girl became pregnant her happiness and ecstasy were worth seeing. She kept hugging and shaking me saying 'I am going to be a mother! I'm going to be a mother!' That was the first time I asked myself 'Where were you? Why didn't you feel this thrill, this ecstasy?' The response was: Remember when you would get up at five in the morning to clean the house and after making breakfast leave by bus for the university; then at 11 o'clock having finished with the university go by bus and on foot to your office at Samanabad, finish at the office at 6 o'clock, go by bus to Lakshmi Chowk; then the housework, the threats of the in-laws—'We'll have you picked up, kidnapped'; reading till late preparing for the university. Then in the midst of all this one day I found out that I was pregnant and the day I didn't turn up at the office was the day my child was born.

Our wedding night—what a strange night it was! We were together but as though hiding from each other. We couldn't believe that this unexpected union was taking place. After he had gone to sleep I spent the whole night sitting on the steps thinking—he has only two and a half rupees. How will we manage? The next day I was on the road to the university looking for a job.

Until 1970 my weight was 96 pounds but then the daily headaches started and the low blood pressure; my hands and feet would get twisted. My doctors were very gracious and kind. They had guessed that all these illnesses had a psychological basis. Often they would just sit me down in the room and ask how I was. They would look at the state I was in and talk to me in such a way that I would burst into tears. They were great doctors. Seeing me weeping they would go on talking to make me weep even more. I would cry my eyes out, jabber away, and they would see my pulse returning to normal. In the midst of my tears I would be smiling. I would apologize for my behaviour and these kind friends would not even charge me any fees, but would come to see me off at the door. Then, seeing my nature and my condition, they prescribed many injections and medicines and warned me that I would have to continue with this until my weight went up to 120 pounds.

I had to struggle a lot to free myself from my own prison. There was a gap between my teeth, a big gap. Whenever I appeared on television people would ring up and harass me. 'Why don't you have a tooth inserted?' The elders would say 'No, no it's a sign of luck.' For a long time I went on listening to all this. One day I went to the dentist and had this sign of the gods removed.

I had very long hair. When Mother would make me sit on the chair and wash my hair I would cry my eyes out. It took hours to untangle my fine hair. I would put it up in a bun for the office and decorate it with jasmine flowers. But even that was not acceptable. So one day I picked up the scissors and chopped off my plait myself. From then on I always had my hair short so that it wouldn't fall on to my face while reading and writing.

When I had reached the fortieth step of my life I discovered that all those things that you don't use any more protest against their neglect in the same way as you. At the age of 22, having given birth to two children, I had decided that this was all the family I needed (even though at that time family planning had not become fashionable). So one day my gynaecologist friend operated on me and revealed the story of my internal shrieks. It was then that I wrote the poem 'Farewell to Uterus'.

After the operation I spent three weeks in the hospital and during this period I read some 50 books on menopause and hysterectomy. In every book it was written 'Women become irritable, quick to get angry; they get fat, they lose interest in sex. They become dry, they become like rotten vegetables. They develop beards and moustaches.'

Many of us women who have been through this stage, laugh at how divorced book learning is from reality. In order to keep a woman enchained even medical principles are devised and the changes in a woman's body are regarded less with wonder and more as a disease. In olden days when the razor blade had not been invented the most lucrative profession was a barber's. Today the most popular profession is to do with women: hysteria, childbirth, birth control, abortion, hysterectomy, weight loss, psychological illnesses, and plastic surgery. All these things flourish in the name of women's health and beauty.

In the giddiness of youth—for those who have experienced it, I certainly didn't—there are many things of which you remain unaware. You only value them as you mature: love of serenity, love of maturity, or the respect which people of all ages have for your grey hair and your lined face. The age which books keep frightening us of, that age has given me a lot of confidence and appreciation. On the other hand, as in Tagore's story, some women die to prove that they are still alive because the word 'widow' gets attached to their name. Everywhere, in the column for age, the letter for unfortunate is circled against your name. During the wedding rituals each one is called up by name but you stand aside yourself. Travelling overseas you notice a husband and wife being affectionate to each other, feeling even closer in old age. You step aside yourself. In the festivities of friends everyone is making merry. They are calling you. But their expressions of familiarity seem forced. There are whispers, shared looks, that tell stories. If you ask anyone to drop you home or to pick you up then there's hell to pay. It spreads like wildfire that so and so dropped you home yesterday.

God, seas, mountains, all stand apart, listening to the tales that come from the lips of people.

Chapter Ten
Uncrowned Zarrin

Although a mushaira is a cultural event, to keep this cultural event within the bounds of culture is not easy. Every individual, every thinking being, has a different set of cultural norms but there is always a basic level of respect and politeness. However, for some unknown reason, in the case of poets this is interpreted in a different way. Irresponsibility, dishevelled hair, dirty clothes and drunken behaviour has since long been accepted as the poet's way. But now the tastes are different. When you ask poets to a mushaira one calls out: 'Please pick up cigarettes', or 'It's a long journey, do get some fruit', or 'Get some plain paans with aniseed and *mulathi*'. Then the meals—more hens must die from mortification at being on the plates of gluttons than by being slaughtered! In connection with the order of reading, the poet's status is recognized according to who read after whom and before whom. Try to arrange it as best as you can but poets will always be disgruntled about not being positioned according to their status. There was a time when the tonga fare, paan expenses, travelling expenses, and payment for participating in the mushaira would be properly noted down on paper and presented for reimbursement. (I have seen Josh Sahib's bills.)

With regard to women's participation in mushairas one practice that became common was of women being considered as poets on the basis of their voice. Naturally the magic wand of someone's poetry was needed to pass them off as poets and in this process there were many occasions for moaning and groaning before poets like us could say toward the end of the night, oh, well, she was worth watching.

Such attitudes towards women damaged the impressions regarding all women poets. This could be remedied; the issue was one of time. It was not easy to participate all night long in a mushaira and go to the office the next morning. Then the kinds of taunts you had to put up with.... When going to a mushaira in some small town people would say: 'Here come the dancing girls, the show is about to begin!' On top of that the organizers of the mushaira would not call the poetesses because of their status or esteem but rather to make it more interesting and colourful. While issuing their invitation they would insist that the poetess should also be a singer. If the mushaira was outside the country it was the same request: 'Three poets and one poetess. If they are all singers it would be better.'

For a poetess to be a singer became a necessity. Necessity is the mother of invention. Poetesses began to be manufactured, made to order in return for love, friendship, a regular barter. It didn't matter that they were neither fish nor fowl, or how hard their creators had to work, getting them to understand each line of verse and pronounce it correctly; to teach them the etiquette of the mushaira. They would advise them to talk less so as not to give the game away. And if the aim of the mushaira is to produce a ghazal then those who live their lives constantly in fear of the fish getting away must be very ambitious indeed.

To read a verse tunefully is itself a discipline but now with mushairas having become cheaper than mujras, the former are more popular. This is because not only will you be regarded as cultured but it's an opportunity for carousing to boot. As it is, for one night the singer has to be paid separately for hordes of accompanying musicians as well as accommodation at a good hotel. Whereas all that the poor poets need is to be asked with affection and they come along willingly. Contented by nature they'll bless you if you feed them. Otherwise, having participated in the mushaira, they'll make their own way home. This is the situation also with the mushairas in our neighbouring country.

Perhaps Urdu is the only language whose poets pride themselves on being illiterate. Many poets, despite insisting on remaining illiterate, claim to churn out an average of four ghazals and four *nazms* every month. Some poets have the habit of writing every evening from five to nine; reading is not compulsory. Then there are some individuals who don't consider themselves to be poets unless they have written one ghazal every day, be it good or bad. There are also some individuals whose ghazals we used to hear in mushairas in our childhood and we continue to hear the same ghazal in our old age, patiently and humbly. A new breed has entered the mushaira scene and that is the breed of columnists and editors of literary pages. Just as at independence some people changed into Syeds, in the same way there are those who turned into poets before our very eyes. One ghazal and an introductory couplet or two may be their entire output but they too are accepted into the cultural circle and flit about like chirping bulbuls reading ghazals. The hosts do them a favour but there is a *quid pro quo* for everything. On the one hand, through the literary pages of the newspapers Jupiter turns their work into masterpieces, because those who preside over and organize the mushaira are deputy commissioners of the district and even announce: 'Today there are some eminent poets participating'. On the other hand, as they preside over the mushaira so sharing out the rewards is also their responsibility. Their photographs with the poets are published and bring honour to them and it also happens that many of these deputy commissioners become poets themselves and some famous singer sings their work and makes them immortal. It is not just women who have poetic pretensions. Many men too have *diwans* to their name and have been regarded as poets of the first rank, without feeling the slightest bit ashamed of having depended on other people's work.

Vanity publishing has been taken to its heights to some extent by writers who had iron mongers' shops and factory permits, or were heads of government departments, or by the grace of God had some other position of authority. Subsequently writers started going off to Dubai. If not themselves, then their kith and kin went and started fulfilling the dreams of their brothers and sisters. They also created stipend holders who at every opportunity would sing their praises and convince everyone that this is the only person who is producing literature. Or else there were those poor souls who were touting their own wares and promoting themselves by setting up organizations and creating piles of their own books.

The trend of totting up your appearances in current articles also started. You would check if your name had appeared in such and such an article, speech, broadcast, supplement, or discussion. And if so then in what order. And who was critical. If someone was critical then you unleashed on them your pet columnist or feature writer. If this wasn't possible then there was always the 'Letter to the Editor'. If you couldn't even manage that then you had no business to count yourself among those jostling for position in the literary arena.

Writers resort to many tricks while jostling for position. If the writer is a poet and, heaven forbid, a commissioner or high-level income tax officer of a district, then critics will be falling all over them; there will be functions in their honour; special issues; and the writer in return will be passing on advertisements, paper quotas, gifts of ration depots. The title of patron of literature is theirs already. If you talk to the publishers who are publishing their work about publishing the work of some poor but good poet then you'll be told: 'The market is down. No one is reading poetry these days.' Ask them how has their work been published then? The reply: 'Their own department has bought the lot, after all.' Selling books on the basis of the author's autograph was also tried. The most books that were sold were by an officer—fat *seths* carried away bundles, like boxes of sweetmeat. In front of our eyes a minister appointed a writer on the salary of a section officer and got ten books written in two years; having got them translated into Arabic and Persian, courtesy of the department, he then got the distinction of being an international writer.

A distinction was also got by one of our seniors who wrote to the head of state that he hadn't received the president's medal as yet—and his wish was fulfilled. The distinction of doctorate is also obtained by those professors who take the notes of their bright students and get them published under their own names; and also by those students who convert their professor's class notes into a book and get them published instantly. On the other hand, those Pakistanis who get awards, and that too international awards, have to listen to all kinds of taunts and accusations in their own country. One lifetime would not be enough to listen to them all because people are so bold and if it is a woman then no part of her life is safe from scandal or blame.

Of those who rely on other people's writing there is one special class which includes actresses. Novels are published under their names and with their permission. There are also those women—wealthy begums—who can buy ghazals and novels, rather buy the writer of the ghazal and novel too and, having got what they paid for, enjoy them under the covers as well. Then there is one class of women who don't even exist. Under their names, half-baked novels are written by men and sold or kept in cheap libraries, as many as ten copies in each. Boys and girls of the neighbourhood underline the mushy phrases of these novels and fuel their romances because they are very effective in expressing their sentiments. These novelists are often writers who are unemployed after having worked in films. They sell trashy romantic stories in the name of women's novels and pander to adolescents who are sitting at home after having passed their matriculation.

Who compels them to write these novels? Their stomach and the publisher. The publisher knows that novels sell in thousands and a novel written under a female pseudonym sells like hot cakes in stalls in railway stations and kiosks and is the best means of passing time for every girl who is sitting at home. It is only with the help of such novels that girls who are waiting for proposals can endure their greying hair and, by immersing themselves in the characters of the novels, accept the four walls of the house as their fate and wash away the stains of their misfortunes. But these tragic stories, written under pseudonyms to titillate others, are revolting unless they provide some benefit to society.

I remember doing songs, features, speeches, compering for radio and television for Rs 10 in the beginning. At that time you would get Rs 10 for every programme on the radio for which you now get Rs 50 or 100. Television also started at Rs 50 while now you get Rs 150 for compering. In those days when I needed money I translated children's books. At the rate of eight annas per page you would get Rs 300 for a book. Mushairas and sundry work would cover the necessities of life among which were summer and winter clothes for the children.

Sometimes a publisher would say: 'Take half the money up front and half later'. But you would feel loathe to break up the amount. You would think why not have some patience and take the entire sum afterwards when the work is done. Then it could cover so many needs. This is where you would lose out. One publisher gave me quite a thick book to translate. He was also in a hurry to get it back. His office was in Rawalpindi. Every week I would send him the pages that had been translated by PIA and he would have them typed out. I translated the 700-page book in three or three and a half months. Within fifteen days of the translation being completed the book was published. I only found out when I saw it in the bookstalls. With great excitement I opened it. What a surprise! My name wasn't there! When I complained to the publisher and demanded my money, he said: 'There were so many mistakes in your translation that I had to get them corrected by someone else. To credit you would not have been appropriate.'

I told him: 'Then you should have credited the person who had done the corrections; and tell me also who it is.' But all these questions and allegations were an everyday occurrence for him, getting the work done in the cause of revolution and then doing a 360-degree turn himself so you would be left flabbergasted. I wrote a letter of protest to the embassy through which the work had come asking for my money. They replied saying that the publisher had already taken the whole amount in lump sum, including the payment for translation.

The same thing happened to me several times.

In the cause of revolution another publisher arrived with a list of books. I agreed to do one. The book was typed as it was written. During this period he went off somewhere. The typist needed money and asked me for it. I gave it to him as it was for the cause of revolution. When the publisher returned I asked him for the typist's bill along with my money to which he replied: 'What do *you* need money for?' Expenses and income were both swallowed up. When I sent him a legal notice through a lawyer then the partisan of revolution turned up begging for mercy. Who needs such publishers?

One publisher took a manuscript after much persuasion. When the book was published he sent me a ten-year contract to sign. I told him: 'I can only sign a contract for one edition—in ten years there will be ten editions. I can't do it.'

'I use the same contract for all the major poets,' he replied. 'If you don't agree that's up to you.'

I got the books from him and sold 1000 copies in five months. Then another publisher asked permission for a second edition. He seemed very decent and would come to all the literary gatherings. I gave him permission for one book. May God forgive him—until his dying day he kept on saying: 'Only a few copies are left now.'

Another publisher very affectionately and with great insistence got me to translate a book. It sold like hot cakes because the moment it came out the rumour spread that it would be banned. It's now twenty-five years since it was banned but it is still available under the counter. For me, however, the same reply: 'What a loss! The police confiscated the whole lot!'

There are many publishers who don't even need your permission. They are not in the habit of publicizing themselves. They don't bring the book into the market: from the printing press it goes straight to the libraries. You never come to hear of it!

However, I did come across one or two exceptional publishers. Their honesty seems suspect when compared to the cheats. They surprise you by giving you the payment for the second edition without asking and by keeping the royalty payments going.

There is another breed of publishers who are reputed to be saints but behind the scenes their entire extended families flourish in the shelter of this saintliness. The concrete in the foundations of their 12- and 14-bedroom houses is made from the work of those writers who have died struggling for their daily bread. But things never change. Like every revolutionary movement the revolt of the writers against the publishers vanishes like foam. One eminent Urdu woman writer who lives in India came to Pakistan after 27 years. She added up her royalty which came to a minimum of 60 lakh rupees. Hats off to our publishers—they didn't give her one anna but denied it outright! She tried ringing the bell of justice but came away with bloodied hands.

When I return home my writing bears witness in a different way: this almirah—from the royalty of such and such book; this toaster—from participating in a mushaira; this sofa—from translating such and such a book. What a montage: book, knowledge, sofa, toaster, translation. All that is left are dreams, you, us, and me.

Chapter Eleven
Discreet Laila

The Czechoslovakian poet, Jaroslav Seifert says in one of his poems that love is so amazing that even if the whole world turned upside down you would still find somewhere or the other, on some patch of green grass, two lovers sitting, holding hands, their heads close to each other. Love goes through many stages, but one-sided love is a terrible thing, whether you are the one making the advances or the one rejecting them. Breaking off is so painful, yet there are these pages too....

One page is across the ocean....

I was only participating in a conference there. Busy from morning to evening, I had to give four speeches in one day. The translator would convey each speech to the audience. It was the first day. Impressed by my speeches he came over to my table, started asking me questions, my room number. He walked me to my room, then came back to my room at night and talked to me about himself. He and his wife were always quarrelling; he was quite fed up. He wanted to know how men and women fall in and out of love, especially in the East. We started talking and continued till late into the night. The next morning he telephoned to wake me up. I got ready and opened the door—there he was, waiting for me. In the dining hall I went towards a chair—he was standing there ready to seat me. I would go towards the dais and he would bound across to welcome me. I began to descend the stairs—he approached, extending his hand. I came down with him. While boarding the bus I bent down to pick up my luggage—his hand was there—he picked up my luggage. I explained to him and he understood. He realized that it was only a passing friendship. In just a few days the hour of parting forever would be upon us. But it was as though in these few days he had expressed all the longing of a lifetime—all the romance, all the intimacies—without having said a word, without any confessions or expectations, by not coming to leave me at the airport. He said I can't see you go. I keep imagining that you are in the conference. And perhaps it will happen that twenty years from now you and I will meet at some airport. And perhaps only after talking we will recognize each other because both you and I will have grown old.

Those who come from there say that after having divorced his wife he had decorated his room by putting up my photographs. If I went there again would I be able to return his favours? But he snatched this opportunity away too just as he had snatched away the opportunity of saying goodbye.

I met a delegation from his country at another conference. We talked about everything; at each sentence my ears longed to hear his name in some context or the other. My desire grew. I asked: 'And what's he doing?' Pin drop silence—'He's dead.'

'Dead? How?'

'It was something to do with his brain. He suffered for two days, then didn't talk again.'

That is true, he never spoke again, he never even said goodbye to me....

...And the one who wrapped himself in the cloak of dumb devotion for thirty years, where should I look for *his* favours and how should I understand them? He neither married, nor will he do so. He didn't say anything, nor will he do so. He didn't and will not forget. He visited rarely and that is how it will be; coming after one or two months, perhaps ten months or a year, telling me about himself, talking about literature, going over all that had happened to me during the past year. If I asked how do you know? He would reply: 'So, is it not true?' He never allowed his emotions to get the better of him in any matter. But yes, when he was restless he would stand up. If he became restless while driving a car he would let go of the steering wheel. If he was sick he would write down my number for the nurse—when I would reach the hospital the nurses would come to see me in amazement: 'He's such a strange patient, he doesn't let anyone come near him! If anyone does come he drives them out in a fury. But he has called you at home and asked you to come.' I knew that his diffidence was the distinguishing feature of his behaviour and his attachment. There are some vines which grow by spreading along the ground. You can stake them to make them straight but they fall down again.

...And then there was one who was even more reticent. But only when it came to expressing his emotions. Otherwise, his eloquence would make even a river pause to admire his style. I could predict all the shades of his adoration. But when he said to me: 'Tonight, in my sleep, I called out your name', I was furious. This I had not foreseen. He fell silent. Moved to another city. Changed his ways. I hear that now he no longer declares to a woman: 'Tonight, in my sleep, I called out your name.'

And this one...he neither called out my name in sleep nor when awake. But spent a lifetime in restlessness. I would be transferred abroad; he would complete his job willy-nilly and follow me—from the airport straight to my room. He would talk, and be content. Then he would say: 'Now I will go to my wife and kids.' Pretending not to have heard, I would give him advice. He would listen to me, even act upon it. When he would come to me impatient, a stern look from me would quell his fire. What did he get? He would say: 'A mother's love, support, affection, advice, I get it all from you. When I feel helpless I come for support from you.'

He left because he had become too dependent on me. His search and attempts to nurture eastern sweetness in English wives had brought him back to his country. The English wife could not live in the country and went back with her children and he exclaimed: 'Why does the soil call out to me if I keep having to go back!' He put this question to my English face and my Eastern heart explained to him that life is not simply a drawing room or a party. Then for the first time he sat on a *peerhi* and tasted my fresh *phulkas* and *shami kebabs* and his life flashed before his eyes. He saw the distances that were in those relationships where he had committed to lifelong partnership, and compared them with the relationships which had no name. Then he wept bitterly over his disappointments. So once again I hid my face and smothered him in motherly love and he became calm. From across the seas the telephone would ring—every time he would promise to come the following month and then postpone it. I got his leave sanctioned myself. He wrote to his wife that he was coming and I put him on the plane. He left the key to one of his almirahs with me and told me as he was leaving: 'At every crisis I would write a letter to you but I could not send them. Go and read them before they remove my stuff.'

The house was emptied long ago. Those who wanted to take the stuff took it away. Those who opened the things must also have opened the almirah and must have destroyed the letters thinking them to be rubbish. I didn't have the heart to see my face in the words I had chosen not to hear.

But you can't solve anything by closing your ears. Before he died he had given my address to a friend of his: he wanted to keep me abreast of his last journey.

The stories of those who die are so long. Those who for years would arise in the evening; who were beautiful, young, worshippers of beauty, wise, would go straight to the heart of the matter, what did they want out of life? A little freedom: to talk, to sit with someone by the side of the canal or under the shade of a tree, laughing innocently or cooling their feet with the water's caress and making conversation; to recite verses and weep; to lose themselves in love or let themselves go. Such small desires. Such simple longings. The dreams of a simple life. What a short preface and what a brief story. But one died coughing blood and brought the days of my youth face to face with death. Another tried to compensate for his own deprivations by loving my children. When he got his salary his first expenditure was on flowers for my children which he would bring in a rickshaw. He was exceedingly fond of my children. He would shower their faces with so many kisses that my eyes would fill with tears. Then, falling silent, he would leave. The following month once again he would be there with gifts of flowers and tears. He fell sick. Not finding me or my children near he slit his throat with a razor. He was a human being; he couldn't cut through the vein entirely and was in agony in the hospital. I was guilty and yet I didn't go. How could I meet him? Like men do, I put him out of my mind and went my way.

...He was so fond of children that he would get them to call him Uncle. What a strange man! He loved his sister, but not as much as he loved me. He would share the most insignificant domestic details with me. He was married twice, to foreign women. Neither one had worked out because he was a dervish by temperament. If any guest came to the house he would get perturbed. If he was alone he would get melancholy. People called him miserly, but every Eid he would walk over from wherever he was to give my children *eidee*. He would pester me to cook for him. And it was during one of these moods that he went away forever from my house.

He was the heart and soul of abstract art but in poetry he was fond of Rilke. He used to hobnob with writers and artists. He believed there should be no hypocrisy among friends. He didn't like harsh words and strong perfumes. He was searching inside himself and in the world's heart for the bird that wants to build its nest, that doesn't want to fight.

...He was very handsome, fair in complexion. He used to recite poetry passionately and drank a lot too. He refused to get married although many women were in love with him. Many of them were ready to marry him. He adored children. He sacrificed the spring of his days to alcohol and fell ill in the winter of regrets. He took to his bed and never got up until they came to take away his bier. Who was there at his funeral? The same handful of friends: two women and ten men watching his grave being dug. The man who talked of being faithless after reading other people's letters had fallen in love with death so quickly.

...He was very dark. But he thought of himself as handsome. He had a beautiful voice and knew how to recite poetry. He would string words like pearls and pluck music out of them like a *jal tarang*. He had mastered the cadences of Urdu, Hindi—including the Hindi spoken in films—Sanskrit, Persian, Arabic, English, Punjabi, and music. His memory was such that the river's flow was nothing as compared to it and the verses he could recall would soothe the mind. He was obsessed with love. By relating tales of his fictitious past loves to every woman he would try and convince her that she should also love him in the same manner. When matters progressed from platonic love to physical intimacy the girls would run away. In platonic love it was only clouds of words that would dissipate allowing these girls to get their personal work done such as writing poetry, making a name for themselves in the literary world or on radio and television, or getting access to someone. He understood their compulsions too. All those who work in these organizations understand compulsions and satisfy their own through these women and by having relations with them. He was educated, not like all the others. He would say things politely. If it looked as though it was not going his way he would change the topic. Talent was ingrained in the sinews of his body. He would relate these amazing dreams: about over powering spirits, or spirits coming in the night to wake him. If all these dreamy stories did not melt the beloved he would paint a new picture, seeking to gain attention by relating the moving story of his wife's illness, accompanied by weeping and breast beating. To get attention this man approached both men and women and returned fulfilled. But more than all desires is that which is associated with the sexual arena. Perhaps this desire was his life's tragedy. Perhaps that is why, failing in his attempt to express love, he collapsed. The ten days in hospital were all he had to change from being unfulfilled to fulfilled but instead he succumbed to the wounds of a death that he had not wished for.

Sapped by death was he too since many years, the one who would come to meet only after 10 p.m. Who would listen to poetry, declaim, insist on strolling in the moonlight, insist on eating paan and then demand that I come to leave him home, so that his wife would not get mad at him for returning so late. Seeing my face, she would be reassured that he hadn't been keeping such bad company after all that the front door should be shut in his face. Who knows what star of trust was inscribed upon my forehead that was visible to these wives. Why else was it that the race of men all thought that I could be a shoulder to cry on at every emotional crisis and the wives of these very men, finding their husbands with me, would feel reassured and secure.

When the cold season begins the body is so feverish—there is such a difference between external and internal temperatures. During sex in this season the eyes and the lips tell a different tale. Like the East Wind, like the wind that doesn't touch the body, he struggled for many years to live inside me as he wished. He was the author of this story and the protagonist too. He was so needy; telling everyone his story made him happy. He was very selfish. Like the siren he would invite each one to the island of his ego and then turning his hungry eyes towards the world conjure up a show. He said very little but each aspect of his behaviour had an eloquence. And he whose ways were so boring and appearance so-so and who was reasonably intelligent, when his secret doors were opened, they revealed the blazing fires of youth which he had buried thirty years ago thinking that desires—like girls—are better off buried if their future begins to look dim.

First he used to be afraid to laugh, to talk, to enter into casual chatter. But then to bring some light into the murky forest of life he picked up the trusty stick of self-reliance, clearing roads and trails and lighting each with the lamps of his dreams. For many years he lived with poets and poetry and forgot that the island in which he existed was reality. One day he erased all those trails and roads like the text on a slate, not with tears, but the oil with which he used to light the lamps. Then he wrapped himself in a yellow robe and went back to the island.

Every relationship doesn't court the enmity of being recorded. To ignore a relationship is also a form of faithfulness. That which surreptitiously strengthens you from inside without your knowing; not allowing discretion to change into indiscretion but keeping such a strong hold on you that at every moment you feel its alert presence watching over you. When beings as fickle as the sun's rays fall into these depths they too forget their way back.

In the silent reveries of these nameless faces even dreams do not enter. One dewdrop does not distinguish itself from another, a ripple is nothing on its own; it enters into me and memory's flow does not allow the floating faces to be washed up on the shore.

It's a different matter that the cross of Yaqut the Abyssinian is hung around the neck of every Razia Sultana.

Chapter Twelve
The Woman with the Whip

There is a poem by the American poet David Ray titled *The Card-Players**

After Cezanne

How we envy their not caring,
   their sculptural crossing of legs,
their idle tossing of cards!

When they get up they are satisfied
as if from work. They rub
   their hands,
   adjust belts,
jingle change in their pockets, and
see that their wives have been loyal
   in their absence.

Many of my friends and elders have been drinking continuously and regularly for the last forty years, but always in somebody else's house or at some common meeting place. They profess that their families have no idea that they drink alcohol. If you ask them, why not indulge in this carousing in your own house, they reply: 'The wife says I won't allow alcohol to be served in my house.' In other words, it is fine if someone else's house bears the disgrace.

Alcohol has its own etiquette. One person may have something sweet after a peg, another may have yoghurt; some

---

*From *The Touched Life: Poems Selected and New*, The Scarecrow Press, 1982, © 1982 & 2009 by David Ray.

go for pickle while others prefer salty snacks, nibbling at everything from Nimco to cute faces. In Pakistan and India, drinking is more like gluttony. May God bless those who prohibited it. Now people who drink alcohol in a refined manner are rare; instead, you see people falling over it as if they were starved. Thankfully, the days of being caught or having someone sniff your breath or undergoing a medical test at night and then being in the news the next day are gone. Otherwise, this same caravan of pilgrims had a thousand remedies in its pockets. One would eat a guava before leaving, another a banana; some would eat paan. The English also helped by inventing special drops: you just put them into your mouth and the smell of alcohol would vanish—the dread of *shariah* punishments did one good thing at least! The poets who would be drunk the whole day and could not go to any discussions or interviews without downing a quarter bottle could drink to their heart's content by buying it in the black from their Hindu or Christian 'relatives' but the uncertainty about the supply was and is still such that the more you can down in the shortest time the more satisfaction it gives.

Previously it was all quick work: you whipped out your 5-rupee note, bounded across to the restaurant for a glass, got some water from the *sabeel* outside and the alcohol flowed till ten in the night. For those still thirsty there were new avenues: one would go to the Cantonment, another to Gulberg, a third to those dens where the alcohol does not stop flowing. If you tried to take someone home by force, they would jump off the moving vehicle. Some were so stubborn they would go off on foot; the next day you would find that instead of reaching home they were in Sheikhupura!

Our children will be amazed to hear that there were once freedoms in Pakistan: at two in the morning sitting by the canal; some are reciting poetry, some are voicing their appreciation; there are people drinking; beer bottles tied with string are cooling in the water; night is participating too with its silences and its plaints; no one is there to round you up claiming that you are being rowdy, nor is there any news of improper conduct. On moonlit nights, the hillocks of Lawrence Gardens would be full of courting couples. The footpaths of Regal Commercial Building and the university would be alive the whole night with the talk of artists and youth. No girl would be raped, there was no police patrolling in the night. Certainly those who were completely drunk would be carted off by the police. When they had recovered their senses, they would give the telephone number of someone who could bail them out. The phone would always ring at two or three in the morning. You would have to go willy-nilly, bail them out, and drop them home.

The telephone would also ring in those days in connection with another loving ritual. There was no direct dialling then. A call would be booked, a ghazal recited, and you would get the pleasure of hearing new verses. There would be sincerity in the conversation and kindness, no sarcasm or hypocrisy, no resentment. Nowadays sarcasm is an essential requirement for stories and jokes to be funny. Laughing and joking is not part of our tradition. Perhaps because we are not accustomed to hearing the truth. In Urdu dramas too the jester is the only one who speaks the truth, not the ordinary character. Why? Is it because the bell of truth does not ring inside us?

Sometimes it would not be the ring of the telephone but that of the doorbell. It is someone who's totally sozzled. 'You did say come at your convenience so we can sit and chat.'

'*Arre* it is 2 a.m.!'

'Oh, come on, what difference does it make if it is 2 a.m. or 2 p.m.?'

The doorbell rings. It is a very senior, very dear poet friend. A literary session begins; the kids wake up with the noise. I go back to them. But it goes on till the morning call to prayer.

It is afternoon. The tub is filled with bottles of beer. Freshly fried *qatlammas* and *naan* stuffed with *qeema* are being served. All the senior and junior writers are together without any discrimination on the basis of age. It is all so civilized—today at my house, next week at someone else's. Thus, every Sunday (in those days Sunday was the weekly holiday) the pupils would be learning from their masters the way to socialise and the etiquette of the mehfil. Sometimes Jami would be under discussion, sometimes Iqbal or Bulleh Shah.

Look at how it is today—if someone offers to be the host then he is stuck with it forever. The wives of the rest are too delicate: they can't cook, they can't serve alcohol at home. If they accompany their husbands, then there is no need for a jailor: 'That's enough, you're not having a second peg!', 'Look at him! At her house he's even clearing away the plates; at home even a glass of water must be brought to his seat!' What can the poor women do? This is all the culture they will get from reading *Behishti Zevar* and watching television dramas!

There is one thing that India and Pakistan have in common: where there is drink two hotheads will surely get into a fight. They will always promise that this time nothing will happen but there they go again. Urdu literature and its writers are a funny lot. Some of the poets who have written reams on drinking have never even tasted alcohol. While Urdu and Farsi poetry reeks of references to alcohol, prose has kept away from it. The fear of being hauled up for questioning in front of assemblies is there not just in our country but also in a country like America, where it has prevented a woman from becoming attorney general.

Drunkenness manifests itself in various guises. Here is someone clutching the wall and announcing: 'The taxi is free.' Another is listening to his own verses being sung and weeping his eyes out. Then there is the one who can't find his own house. Or the one who tosses his drink at the sea exclaiming: 'Here boy, you also drink.' And there's the one who is messing up your drawing room or courtyard, bringing up everything that was drunk. One is lying in a heap, fast asleep, refusing to go home.

There were some people who would come over the moment it was evening, greet you, sit at your table and without having said a word it was clear what they had come for. With inflation their demands increased. And yet some continued to insist that the price of a bottle had remained the same.

There were also some dear friends in the days gone by who, when they got their salaries on the first of the month, would find their fellow drinkers waiting to drink their share, to take their pocket money. What a bunch! They would spend half their salary on their friends and half on repaying past loans and then get a new line of credit.

But the friends who take the cake are the ones who've been drinking every day for a lifetime, and heavily too, but not from their own pocket. Their fans and friends give it to them, or else they have such a delightful way of asking that the one who is asked feels honoured to oblige.

There is no dearth of poets such as these in offices. If they went to the office, it was only to show their face. And there were a few remarkable officers who would prevent the others from reprimanding these poets in any way (this is about the officers of twenty years ago, not of today). They would say that the office would go down in history only because such and such distinguished writer worked there. Now, the moment any big writer steps into the office all the pygmies are there in a shot, hurling accusations and pulling the writer down.

In all these scenes my role was sometimes as hostess, sometimes as the lady of the house, or in the next room with the children as their mother, or sometimes as the woman cracking the whip. The latter was a role I had to play often. While talking loosely, men love to pepper their language with swear words and once they have downed a few pegs their cloak of refinement slips off. Then you have one arguing in a loud voice, another making a speech, someone hurling abuses and one who is throwing up. To put a halt to such moments I would have to use my sharp tongue, or even my hand, and those loud mouths who were bragging or making up tall stories would trot back to their own houses like trained horses. Decency doesn't allow me to mention the names I would be called then, or even now.

So then how did this taste reach my lips? Picasso once said that art is a lie that makes the truth bearable. In the same way that international conferences and travels taught me to walk with my head up in strange lands and among strangers, it also gradually, in the course of proposing a toast during or after meals, developed in me the taste for wine. During the *kathak* dance a moment comes when the dancer can make the sound of one *ghungroo* only with the tapping of her feet. For me too there came a moment like that: I shattered another chain inside me. Then the hell that broke loose was worse than ever before. 'Are you trying to compete with men?' Apart from my family the sarcastic smiles of my old friends greeted me as well. I like them; they are not hypocritical, sometimes they even talk against me while sitting in my house!

During the period when restrictions were at their height, while inviting a friend over the phone to come over in the evening, or telling them what the purpose of the gathering was, you would say: 'I have *shaljam gosht*, please come'; or you would say: 'I have the book'; or 'A new book has come, please come.'

This is the same tone adopted by some of my elders and my women friends. During the dark days of martial law we went through a lot together; so many of our joys and sorrows are common. Many of my women friends include me in their solitary drinking. They would never touch a drop in public. I respect their principles. But I myself have never liked to be bound by rules. When I came out of the mosque of Cordoba and sat with my sons there was wine in front of us. I said to them:

'My dreams, if you yourselves are unafraid
Then tell me frankly: What is it that people desire?
Those desires in which the intellect prevails
And justice appears like a guardian angel.'

Chapter Thirteen
Sana on the Gallows

There are many things in life which have no relationship as such with the intellect, intuition, philosophy, or feelings. But even then they are accepted as fact. If a bride has to be found then it is said, don't look at the girl, look at her mother. She is going to become like her, so test out and observe the mother first. Now, when I am a mother myself I find such phrases influencing me. My mother—was she like me? Perhaps she was a step ahead of me. No wonder she rebelled against her father and put us into school. Her father said to her: 'Don't come to my house, you are educating girls.' My mother replied: 'I won't come.' My father said to me: 'Don't come to my house, you've married a boy from a different caste, you've thrown off the burqa, you work, you've done your MA.' But my mother also said: 'Don't come to my house.' I said to my son after his marriage: 'You married of your own choice, don't bring your wife to my house. Go feed yourself, earn your own living, support yourself.' So what difference is there between my mother's mother, my mother, and myself?

The conversation between the fashionable working woman—educated, intelligent, with short hair, lipstick and modern clothes—and her maid servant is either totally absent or if not then there is a mismatch and inconsistency in thought and style. The maid servant, ignorant of the secrets of existence and the ego, or the intellectual subtleties in schools and colleges, her face and hands covered in ashes and dirt, but flushed with emotion, talks without hesitation and openly, about her children and husband: '*Arre* Bibi, what do sons give you except more sorrows? They don't bother about you. Girls may suffer joys and sorrows but they come and look you up.'

Upon hearing this, the daughter-in-law, who is so modern that she has kept her parents-in-law in the servants' quarters, rebukes her: 'Don't talk while you are working! Keep your mind on your work!'

Those who educate their sons at MIT look for employment after having retired and, using the excuse of staying busy, maintain their honour, because following traditions has got a stranglehold on every aspect of our lives. We don't accept the fact that relationships change in direction and nature. We fall all over ourselves trying to keep up the pretence of following old customs just to maintain our honour. Everything is for the sake of appearance—that is why the beautiful faces don't know how to express themselves and can't understand or make themselves understood. All around us are walking effigies, who only exist to wear clothes and to eat. What people go through, relationships—what they are and what they should be—these are only learnt through dramas. That is why the customs of *mehndi*, *ubtan* and *rukhsati* have been flourishing for the past twenty years. Why didn't simplicity or learning flourish?

Nevertheless, the circles of despondence have shrunk a lot—the women who were being beaten realized that they were not born just to be beaten. The women who gave foot massages wondered why no one massaged their feet. There was no natural law that said that only they should be giving foot massages. Even the prostitutes sitting on their *kothas* got fed up with the pleasures of men and their own coquetry, while the women sitting at home also got bored with the sameness of life and started shopping in the bazaars to pass the time.

A few days before her suicide, Marilyn Monroe wrote in her diary of her fears. She wondered what it was that made her so afraid. She knew she could still act and yet she was afraid. She, whom men had decided to turn into a sex symbol and had given money and honour, was well-known for her love affairs with prominent men. She had so many abortions that according to a friend of hers her tubes were completely destroyed. But when she died she was alone—perhaps for the first time she was acting according to her own wishes.

'Her own wishes'—a phrase that has entered into a woman's life! From birth, through education, marriage, choice of husband, life, death—those who are locked up in a room and burnt, who are dishonoured and strangled, who are shot for having chosen their own husbands—here too their own wishes are nowhere to be seen. All her life she cooks the man's choice of food, she wears clothes which please the man, jewellery, she gets dolled up, meets people—all within the moorings of her husband's will and permission. As for her own wishes, she is a stranger to them and how they taste.

But then who isn't a stranger? Who is so aware of themselves that they can smell the perfume of their own being? It needs a strong foundation to dispel this estrangement: trust in the other person and to acknowledge wholeheartedly their worth. But here even women don't understand each other, rather they don't believe in their own individuality. In their opinion they are there to serve others. Their belief in themselves and their self-respect is tied up in their relationship with men. They don't believe that they alone are worthy of respect. They feel that the be-all and end-all of their lives is in following the moral and emotional guidelines established by men. They are not allowed to have any connection with what's happening in the world or why it is happening, nor do they realize that they can connect to it.

The word 'protection' has been attached to the female sex. Protecting her love, shelter, future, position in society. It is her fate to be protected by a man. It is to obtain this protection that she goes to pirs for charms and to the tombs of saints; that she holds *milads* and Qur'an *khatms* or *Yasin khatms*; that she is prey to doubts and dangers of all kinds day and night. And when disappointments and bitterness overwhelm her she goes into seclusion at the tombs of saints and stays there from morning to evening, coming home at night to hide her face.

Writing is also considered a sin worthy of hiding your face. The writings of women were never regarded highly. But yes, they are appreciated for their sensationalism and rated accordingly. Norman Mailer said that a woman doesn't make a good writer. But if she becomes a call girl and her stories are written you can get some interesting material. A woman's story has a place of its own. Inside her, as Florence Nightingale said, desire, dreams, enthusiasm, and faults die turn by turn. What dies in the end is her mind. The mind has the power to remain alive without any support. Even if it is repressed it gets sustenance from whatever it encounters. Sorrow—anger—food—are the three companions of loneliness. Look at women writers: they haven't written half of what George Eliot, Jane Austen, Virginia Woolf—the pioneers—wrote. They even had to change their names. In our part of the world, after marriage, many women writers were finished. Was their goal, their personal goal, marriage alone? If it was, then why was one level of fire not missing from their writings? If a man stops writing, the world mourns: what a mind! What went wrong? If a woman stops writing then it heaves a sigh of relief. Now she can follow the true path and be a real mother, housewife, and wife. Such paths have also been shown to us by our great minds such as D.H. Lawrence. Towards the latter part of his life, Sartre was asked: 'You know Simone inside out as a companion. Do you also acknowledge her literary standing?' Sartre had disagreed with many parts of Simone's *The Second Sex*. In our part of the world the husbands of writers—God forgive me—are a strange breed. They aren't happy with her but they can't let go of her either. A woman writer is like the callus on her husband's hand: she bothers him but he doesn't want her to go away either. Sometimes he will become her publicity agent and will make everyone's life—and hers too—unbearable. If she sits behind seven veils and writes in isolation then well and good. Otherwise, experience, the outside world, knowledge, the company of people, observation, all these are of no value, because they themselves, in whichever field they may be working, stay clear of such 'hardships'. What do they know of learning and the way it sets the mind ablaze? This is why, in ancient times, it was forbidden to educate slaves. In Jewish law it is still forbidden to educate women. But Jewish women do study. In ancient Greece only prostitutes were taught because it would add piquancy to the skills with which they entertained men. The other women were left uneducated (just the way all the officials want English-speaking walkie-talkie dolls, not intelligent women, confident of their own intelligence). According to them girls don't want books, they want husbands. In England, Virginia Woolf had to struggle to get access to books. She wasn't allowed to enter libraries, the same Virginia Woolf who they tried to stop from writing about herself and about woman's bodies. She wrote that she would have to wait for such time when men would cease to be shocked at hearing about a woman's body. Walt Whitman warned women pupils against trying to surpass their teachers. The reason is that society is unable to understand the language of women or their point of view. The example of Victoria Woodhull is before us. This is the woman who worked on Wall Street as a stockbroker, who took part in the American presidential elections in 1870, who published the English translation of the communist manifesto in America in 1871. She was the first person (not just the first woman) in history who was jailed in 1872 under the Comstock law. But her activities, movements, and rebelliousness were not appreciated by women themselves, while the men enjoyed it and turned it into a spectacle. Even now women don't vote for other women. They may work in the office together but they will still consider each other as enemies.

Society and men have made decisions on their own and given it the name of nature. The first decision is that the basic purpose of woman's existence is to give birth because that is the purpose of the womb. True, she has a womb. But she also has a mind. Why then is it never said that a woman's basic purpose is to think and use her mind? According to men a woman's fingers are delicate. So why have they not declared that all surgeons should be women so that with such delicate hands performing operations the stitches will be nice and fine? According to men women have beautiful legs. So why hasn't any attention been given to make them into the best athletes in the world?

One training and one quality alone has been held to be the purpose of her creation and that was and is to give birth, to put up with and accept men's sexual needs. If an educated woman works the whole month and earns Rs 3000 even then she has to hear a thousand taunts both within the house and outside. But if an illiterate woman agrees to offer herself to satisfy a man's lust every night then, after earning thousands for one night, she can still maintain the façade of being a decent, respectable housewife during the day. According to d'Héricourt if you compete against men you'll be disgraced. If you give them pleasure you'll get respect; while Virginia Woolf opines that educated women are very ugly and very poor. There are heaps of books which say: 'The great woman is not the one who writes good books, but the one who produces good children.'

Perhaps it is for this reason that until 1973 in America, and perhaps 1980 in France, abortions could not be legalized. Not that abortions didn't take place before then. They were performed regularly and frequently at the insistence of men but men's legal system allowed centuries to go by before giving it legal and constitutional cover. To reach this stage women themselves were a big stumbling block because they had been taught that a woman is not important; what is important is the child that she is carrying. She was only a custodian of the foetus which was growing inside her. And because the foetus was created out of a man's sperm, aborting it was like aborting the man. To what extent the man accepted the paternity of the child and the responsibility was altogether a different matter. Nowhere was it said that the egg was fertilized by the meeting of the cells of both the woman and the man.

The crutch of religion is certainly sought when making laws. In male–female relations every religion has given superiority to men because all religions have been imposed by men and interpreted by them. So men's ideas or laws to do with women are regarded as God's laws. This is why, whether a woman wants to or not, whoever society marries her to, it becomes her legal duty to obey that man and to be ready and willing to have sex at his command. Because sex is directly related to pregnancy, to be ready for pregnancy is part of the law. To be ready for sex according to the husband's wishes is taken as the cornerstone of a wife's devotion; that she make him happy and keep him happy and if she should displease him then be prepared for the most miserable moments of her life. In short, the whole social framework has been set up to prop men up as the source of power. Accordingly, for a woman to be economically independent, or to come on to an equal managerial footing, or for her intellectual standing in society to be acknowledged, are all regarded adversely and a legal environment is created to prevent moves towards equality.

The year 1960 was regarded as a turning point for socialism as well as sex. That is why Norman Mailer claimed that the sexual revolution during that period had fallen into the hands of the wrong people because love was taken to mean not just sex but peace and love of humanity. This was because American youth were against war. They didn't want to burn in the fire of Vietnam. They started growing their hair long, wearing colourful clothes and painting their faces in psychedelic colours. For the first time girls found themselves able to have an intellectual dialogue on the same platform as men. Here another class joined them: the class of Black Americans because the American legal system didn't give them equal opportunities or facilities.

This freedom began to move in another direction: from group sex to experimentation with all kinds of sexual activity. The homosexual and lesbian movement started here because as the

Marxists put it this was the period for experimenting with breaking all sexual taboos. But this movement and this attitude remained confined to one class; forced sex continued and is still there around the world.

All these issues came to mind one by one and I wrote them down during my trip to America. It was a very long trip covering twenty-four universities and requiring me to set off every second day. I have had the habit since a long time to write on the plane, and I write a lot. I enjoy it so much—reading and writing. After a while the airhostess comes herself and takes me to the most comfortable seat, the most secluded. Nuts, wine, pen, paper, space, and anonymity....

CHAPTER FOURTEEN
Eve and the Son of Adam

He used to rummage in my bag and I in his pockets. This was the extent of our trust and respect for each other. Like a wandering deer or a peddler he would go from door to door but would always come home at night; while I, despite all my complaints and lamentation, could not erase the traditions of Sita that were ingrained in me.

When he would go out on the quiet it wouldn't surprise me. And when he left after announcing it to everyone it did not give me any pain. After his death when his effects came back and there was no money in his bank account—even then I wasn't surprised and I didn't try to find out where his earnings of one and a half years had gone.

Like many husbands and wives the two of us, estranged individuals, had become the parents of two children.

My children were very hardy and courageous. I started sending the older one to school alone on a bicycle from the age of seven. The younger one would also go to school on his bicycle at the same age. Their father would go to the office by car and their mother would go in a rickshaw or in the office car.

I translated children's stories at the rate of one rupee a page and did proofreading at eight annas a page. My children and I would sit together around the same table; they would be doing their homework and I my translations or a radio script. I would tell them this work will earn so many rupees; from this we will buy your socks or your books and they would let me work in peace. I would take them in a rickshaw for swimming or to the Arts Council for painting classes.

When there was no servant and the children had a holiday I would lock the door from outside and go to office. I would be anxious the whole day but what could I do? Coming back home my heart would be in my mouth. Once the younger one, while playing with matches, set fire to the bed. The room was filled with smoke. Fortunately, one window was open. When I returned from office, I found him cowering there. He was then five years old.

Another time the older boy, while imitating the stunts of Chinese acrobats, broke three of his teeth. When I returned home, I saw him hiding from me. When he came in front of me he had his hand over his mouth. I removed his hand and saw that his mouth was all bloody. When I asked him what had happened he burst into tears. At that time he was eight years old. I picked him up, got a rickshaw, took him to the doctor. He had fallen so badly that it took the doctor several hours: the roots of his teeth had got shaken.

The duty of bringing my older son back from nursery school had been entrusted to his grandfather. One day I returned from office to find that the child was not at home. I went to the school. On a cold winter's evening the boy was sitting alone on the bench of the school *chowkidar*: his grandfather had forgotten to pick him up.

My children would often heat up their food themselves when they came home. On the orders of a modern woman like me they had even started sleeping in a separate room from an early age. They only told me afterwards how frightened they used to be sleeping alone, which is why they would come to me at all hours of the night. I was very bad. I would tell them to read books. I would make them sit learning the Qur'an. I would not give them pocket money. I would send them to school with a packed lunch. Their father was so good he only gave them love! When I would stop them from playing truant, he would give them permission. He would fulfil all their wrong demands. He was their hero.

Then it so happened that suddenly we got a windfall. The children got motorcycles at that young age, money to spend and discovered all the ways of avoiding their studies. Their books and their mother faded into the background. This carnival lasted for a few years and undid all relationships. I became all alone. I would hear the guffaws coming from the room next door and would sit covering my ears with books. First there were separate households under one roof, then separate houses within one city, then everyone was scattered in different countries.

When the carnival was over, the distances and the responsibility of being parents created many chasms. My children at a very young age had the courage to support themselves. The younger son set himself up in a foreign country all by himself and is today the father of a daughter and a good-hearted human being.

The older son took a long time to emerge from the mirage of sudden wealth and went through many hard knocks. Today, in Spain, when people commend him for his business sense I remember that child who used to get the first prize in painting. He would write poetry, would always come first in swimming but would tell me: 'Ammi, you also take the cake, you are happy just with applause.'

The three lines of a triangle can't meet. If they do it won't be a triangle. If they separate it won't be a triangle either. The three of us—my two sons—and I are like the lines of a triangle.

May my enemies, those tracking my loneliness through arrow slits, continue to prosper, but I am not one of those who say: 'For whom should I beautify myself now?' I am like the woman in Chekhov's story who, having fulfilled her responsibilities, started living for herself and to serve her own people according to their wishes. I have strung every moment like a pearl, a lustrous pearl, on the string of experience. I have studied the faces and tasted the cultures flowing through the alleys of the world. I am a cowardly woman; I can only walk in the shadow of my own confidence. In my family women live long but I have seen them like vegetables: interested only in their likes and dislikes. This is not the be-all and end-all of existence. Yes, to remain, like Simone de Beauvoir and Betty Freidan, active and to continue to write till the very end, that seems to be the key to the enigma of existence.

In the words of Sylvia Plath:

> I'm a riddle in nine syllables,
> An elephant, a ponderous house,
> A melon strolling on two tendrils.
> 'O red fruit, ivory, fine timbers!
> This loaf's big with its yeasty rising.
> Money's new-minted in this fat purse.
> I'm a means, a stage, a cow in calf.
> I've eaten a bag of green apples,
> Boarded the train there's no getting off.*

---

*From *Sylvia Plath: Collected Poems*, London: Faber & Faber Ltd, 1981, © the Estate of Sylvia Plath.

Glossary

Adeeb Fazil: Honours in Urdu Literature.

Al Badr: The paramilitary wing of the Jamaat-e-Islami in Bangladesh (then East Pakistan) that earned infamy for its collaboration with the Pakistan Army against the Bengali nationalist movement in the Bangladesh Liberation War.

Al Shams: A militia force formed in Bangladesh in 1971 by the Pakistan Army.

alam: Processional standard.

aloo parathas: Spiced potato flat bread.

Apa Jan: Elder sister.

Ayat al-Kursi: The verse of the throne (Surah 2 Baqarah: verse 255).

azaan: The Islamic call to prayer.

bait baazee: Verse recitation competitions.

Baji: Sister.

Baqr Eid: Also called Eid al-Adha. A religious festival celebrated by Muslims.

baris: Flat lentil cakes.

Behishti Zevar **(Literally Heavenly Ornaments):** A book specifically written for women by Maulana Ashraf Ali Thanvi, a famous religious scholar. This book gives a list of do's and don'ts for girls and women from the Islamic viewpoint.

besani roti: Chickpea/gram flour flat bread.

biryani: A rice-based dish made with spices, rice and meat/vegetables.

bosky: A fabric which is 100 per cent cotton with a silky feel.

Burhi Ganga: Buriganga River, Burhi Ganga (Brahmaputra), is the main river flowing beside Dhaka city, capital of Bangladesh.

burqa: An enveloping outer garment worn by women for the purpose of cloaking the entire body.

chador: A full-length semicircle of fabric open down the front, which is thrown over the head and held closed in front.

chiks: Fabric and bamboo or reed blinds.

cholay: Chickpeas.

chota: Urdu slang word for young (male) helper, servant or assistant.

Choudhry: Literally meaning 'a holder of four' or 'owner of the fourth part'. Traditionally, the term is used as a title indicating the ownership of ancestral land, but in contemporary usage it is often taken as a surname.

chowkidar: Watchman.

degh: Big copper/aluminium utensils used for cooking large amounts of food.

desi ghee: Butter oil.

dhoti: Long loincloth.

Diwali: The Hindu festival of lights

dobari: Corridor.

Dua-e-Qunoot: Prayer recited in Isha prayers.

dupatta: A long scarf.

Dussehra: A popular festival celebrated by Hindus.

Eid: Festival celebrated by Muslims.

eidee: Money given as a gift to children on Eid.

fatwa: A legal pronouncement in Islam, issued by a religious law specialist on a specific issue.

ghararas: A traditional garment consisting of a pair of wide-legged pants, ruched at the knee so they flare out dramatically, worn with a short, mid-thigh length tunic and a veil.

ghazal: A poetic form consisting of rhyming couplets and a refrain.

ghungroo: One of many small metallic bells strung together to form a musical accessory tied to the feet of classical Indian dancers.

gulli danda: An amateur sport, similar to cricket.

hakim: A person who practices a combination of herbal medicine, homoeopathy, naturopathy, chiropractic and others.

halwa: Types of sweet confection.

hamd: A poem or song in praise of Allah.

haveli: A private mansion.

Holi: Also called the Festival of Colours, is a popular Hindu spring festival.

iddat: A period of waiting that Islam has imposed upon a woman who has been divorced or whose husband has died, after which a new marriage is permissible.

imam: An Islamic leadership position. Often the leader of a mosque and the community.

Isha prayers: Night-time daily prayer recited by practising Muslims. It is the fifth of the five daily prayers.

jal tarang: An ancient musical instrument of South Asian origin.

jalali: Most intense forms of *zikr* (a devotional act often includes the repetition of the names of Allah, supplications and aphorisms from sections of the Quran).

kamarband: A sash for the waist; a girdle loin band.

Kamasutra: An ancient Indian text widely considered standard work on human sexual behaviour in Sanskrit literature written by the Indian scholar Vatsyayana.

kamiz: Long shirt or tunic.

kathak: A form of north Indian classical dance.

khaddar: Coarse thread raw cotton fabric.

khichra: A dish made of wheat, meat (usually beef or mutton, but sometimes chicken or minced meat), lentils and spices.

khutba: The address delivered in the mosque at weekly and annual prayers.

koonda: Special meals prepared on fulfilment of a vow.

kotha: Terrace; brothel.

kurcha: Long-handled metal ladle.

kurta: Loose shirt falling either just above or somewhere below the knees of the wearer, and is worn by both men and women.

laddoo: A sweetmeat.

latha: Fine thread raw cotton fabric.

lota: Small, usually spherical water vessel of brass or copper typically used by Muslims either for mandatory ablutions before prayers, or in the toilet.

majlis: A common term used for a special gathering in remembrance of Hazrat Imam Hussain, the grandson of Prophet Muhammad (PBUH).

makai ki roti: Cornmeal flat bread.

marsiya: An elegiac poem written to commemorate the martyrdom and valour of Hazrat Imam Hussain and his comrades in Karbala.

mashk: A traditional bag for carrying water made out of goatskin.

maulvi: An honorific Islamic religious title often given to Muslim religious scholars or Ulema preceding their names, similar to the titles Maulana, Mullah, or Sheikh.

mehfil: A gathering or evening of entertainment of poetry or concert of Indian classical music.

mehndi: Henna.

milad: Reading of poetry or the praise of Prophet Muhammad (PBUH) in a gathering.

misra tarah: The sample line.

mohajir: Refugee or immigrant or emigrant.

mujra: A form of dance originated by North Indian Muslim courtesans during the Mughal era.

mulathi: Liquorice.

mullah: a Muslim man, educated in Islamic theology and sacred law.

Munshi Fazil examination: Persian diploma course.

mushaira: A poetic symposium. An event where poets gather to perform their works.

naan: A round flatbread made of white flour.

naat: Poetry in praise of Prophet Muhammad (PBUH).

naib tehsildar: Deputy of a tehsildar (revenue administrative officer).

Namaz-e-Janaza: Funeral prayers.

nazm: An Urdu poetic form that is normally written in rhymed verse.

nihari: A stew made from the shank of beef (or lamb) and spices.

nishasta: A fine starchy powder milled from maize and wheat.

niwar: Cotton webbing.

numberdar: Village head.

***Pakki Roti*:** A book written by Ghulam Rasul (1813–1874) in Punjabi prose, recounting the injunctions for a Muslim.

paratha: A flatbread made with whole wheat flour, pan fried in ghee or cooking oil.

patwari: A land record clerk.

paya: A stew made of cow, goat or lamb's skull and feet. *Siri* means the head of the animal and *paya* means the feet of the animal.

peerhi: A low stool to sit on.

phulka: Whole wheat flatbread also known as chapatti or *roti* which is cooked directly on an open flame.

pir: Sufi teacher, spiritual leader.

purdah: A screen or veil. A practice that includes the seclusion of women from public observation by wearing concealing clothing from head to toe and by the use of high walls, curtains, and screens erected within the home.

qanungos: Fiscal officers.

qatlamma: Gram flour *naan* but very thin and very large. It is crunchy and crispy with delicious toppings.

qeema: Minced meat.

Quran khatms: A gathering for completion of the recitation of the Holy Quran.

roti: See *phulka*.

Rukhsati: A ceremony whereby the bride departs to the groom's house.

sabeel: Water stalls.

samosa: A snack of deep fried dumplings stuffed with minced meat, potatoes or cauliflower with peas.

seth: Businessman.

shaljam gosht: A dish made of turnips and meat.

shalwar: Loose pajama-like trousers.

shami kebabs: A small patty of minced beef or chicken and ground chickpeas and spices, which is fried in oil.

shamshan ghat: Cremation ground of the Hindus.

Shariah: Islamic law.

sherwani: A long coat-like men's garment.

Shikasta script: A version of cursive Urdu script (*shikasta* means 'broken').

Sita: Wife of Rama who Hindus believe is an avatar of the supreme god Vishnu. She is esteemed as the model wife.

surma: Collyrium; antimony reduced to fine powder for applying to the eyes.

Tahajjud: A supererogatory prayer.

talaq: Divorce.

tazia: Mourning; glittering replicas of the tombs of the martyr's of Karbala.

tonga: A light horse-drawn two-wheeled vehicle used in India and Pakistan.

ubtan: A cosmetic paste for the skin made from turmeric, sandalwood powder, herbs and aromatic oils.

Urad flour: A type of flour, native to India, which is made by grinding black gram pulses or lentils into a fine powder.

wazifa: A litany of the Divine Names and Attributes of God.

yaar: Informal for 'friend'.

Yasin khatms: A gathering for the completion of the recitation of Surah Yasin, one of the chapters of the Quran.

zina: Extramarital and premarital sex.